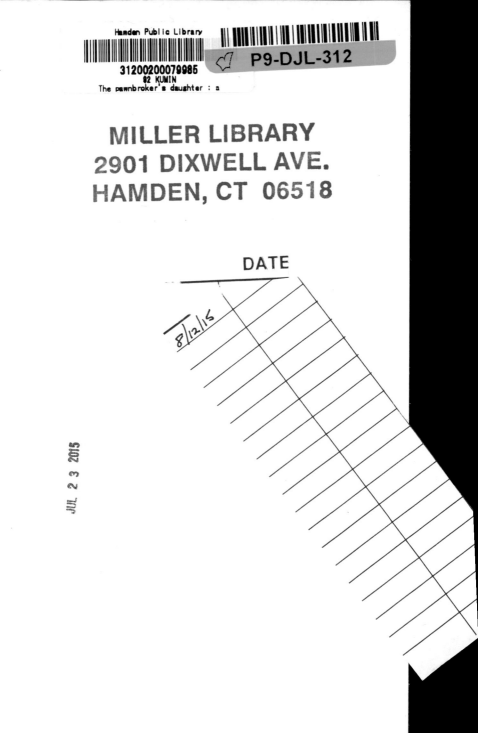

The
Pawnbroker's
Daughter

Also by Maxine Kumin

POETRY

And Short the Season
Where I Live
Still to Mow
Jack and Other New Poems
Bringing Together
The Long Marriage
Selected Poems 1960–1990
Connecting the Dots
Looking for Luck
Nurture
The Long Approach
Our Ground Time Here Will Be Brief
The Retrieval System
House, Bridge, Fountain, Gate
Up Country
The Nightmare Factory
The Privilege
Halfway

NOVELS

Quit Monks or Die!
The Designated Heir
The Abduction
The Passions of Uxport
Through Dooms of Love

ESSAYS AND SHORT STORY COLLECTIONS

Why Can't We Live Together Like Civilized Human Beings?
Always Beginning: Essays on a Life in Poetry
Inside the Halo and Beyond: The Anatomy of a Recovery
Women, Animals, and Vegetables: Essays and Stories
In Deep: Country Essays
To Make a Prairie: Essays on Poets, Poetry and Country Living
The Roots of Things

Maxine at age four on the boardwalk in
Atlantic City, New Jersey. *Kumin Family Photo*

The

Pawnbroker's

Daughter

A Memoir

Maxine Kumin

W. W. NORTON & COMPANY

NEW YORK · LONDON

For information about permission to reproduce selections from this book,
write to Permissions, W. W. Norton & Company, Inc.,
500 Fifth Avenue, New York, NY 10110

For information about special discounts for bulk purchases, please contact
W. W. Norton Special Sales at specialsales@wwnorton.com or 800-233-4830

Manufacturing by Courier Westford
Book design by Mary Austin Speaker
Production manager: Anna Oler

Library of Congress Cataloging-in-Publication Data

Kumin, Maxine, 1925–2014.
    The pawnbroker's daughter : a memoir / Maxine Kumin.
        pages cm
Summary: "From Pulitzer Prize–winning poet Maxine Kumin, a timeless memoir
of life, love, and poetry. Maxine Kumin left an unrivaled legacy as a pioneering poet
and feminist. *The Pawnbroker's Daughter* charts her journey from a childhood in
the Jewish community in Depression-era Philadelphia, where Kumin's father was
a pawnbroker, to Radcliffe College, where she comes into her own as an intellectual and meets the soldier–turned–Los Alamos scientist who would become her
husband; to her metamorphosis from a poet of 'light verse' to a 'poet of witness';
to her farm in rural New England, the subject and setting of much of her later
work. Against all odds, Kumin channels her dissatisfaction with the life that is
expected of her as a wife and a mother into her work as a feminist and one of the
most renowned and remembered twentieth-century American poets"—Provided
by publisher.
    ISBN 978-0-393-24633-9 (hardcover)
1. Kumin, Maxine, 1925–2014. 2. Poets, American—20th century—Biography.
3. Poetry consultants—United States—Biography. 4. Feminists—United States—
Biography. I. Title.

PS3521.U638Z469 2015
811'.54—dc23
[B]
                                                        2015009312

W. W. Norton & Company, Inc.
500 Fifth Avenue, New York, N.Y. 10110
www.wwnorton.com

W. W. Norton & Company Ltd.
Castle House, 75/76 Wells Street, London W1T 3QT

1 2 3 4 5 6 7 8 9 0

for Victor

Contents

The
Pawnbroker's
Daughter

I.

Need Money? See Pete.
Recollections by the
Pawnbroker's Daughter

Maxine and her father, Peter Winokur Sr., on her wedding day,
June 29, 1946. *Kumin Family Photo*

When I was growing up in the 1930s, the first four words I learned to read were *Need money? See Pete.* In that era of carefree smoking, every pack of cigarettes in greater Philadelphia came with a free matchbook, many of them adorned, front and back, with these words. My father Peter owned the biggest pawnshop in the city. He had inherited it from his father, Max Winokur, for whom I was named. According to my oldest brother, Grandfather had first owned a shirt factory until, at the end of World War I, his workers had demanded the right to form a union and when he refused went out on strike. Rather than accede, Grandfather shut the enterprise down. After several lean months he bought a foundering store in the heart of the ghettoized black section of South Philadelphia and named it Federal Loan.

A funny mixture of sybarite and Calvinist, my father left school at the age of thirteen in order to help in the store while his older brother Joseph became the family scholar. Joseph went on to college and law school at the University of Pennsylvania, but despite the degrees he earned, he was never financially successful. Behind the scenes, my father, who was devoted to his older brother, made up the difference. I'm sure this contributed to the tension that escalated between the brothers' wives.

I was aware from an early age how different my mother's upbringing was from my aunt's. Aunt Bea, an only child, grew up in Berlin and Paris. Sixth in a family of twelve children, my mother grew up in Radford, Virginia, a small town where her father owned the general store. When she could be induced to talk about it, her story was an idyll of chickens and rabbits, a family pony, and her father's matched pair of Saddlebreds that he drove in harness.

Music teachers came and went in Radford; my mother, who had shown a precocious ability to pick out tunes on the family upright, took lessons from the time she could sit on the piano bench. She was fifteen when the

Methodist church organist moved away. Although they were the only Jewish family in Radford, she became the official church organist with her father's permission. In addition to Sunday services, she also played for all the church weddings and funerals. When, at eighteen, she came to Philadelphia to live with an older married sister, she enrolled at the Coombs Conservatory of Music. Although unspoken, it was clearly hoped that she would find an appropriate Jewish husband.

She and my father met at a Saturday night party in the suburbs. She was playing the piano when my father burst in jovially and had to be shushed so that the concert could continue. "Who is this haughty dame?" my father is said to have inquired, while my mother glared in his direction. It didn't seem a propitious beginning, but they eloped the following year. Four of us children arrived at explicit three-year intervals. The only girl, I was the last of the line, alternately cosseted and resented by my brothers. I was also the only child born in the house on Carpenter Lane, which my parents had bought just a few months before my birth in June 1925.

The house was a spacious three-story Georgian colonial, built in 1895 next to the commodious property of the convent of the Sisters of St. Joseph, a teaching order. Our house perched on top of two sets of stairs leading to a wide brick terrace. A broad hall opened to a living room, a music room containing my mother's Steinway, a dining room, breakfast room, large kitchen, pantry, and laundry. Upstairs there were five bedrooms and three baths.

At the age of five, over my father's mild objections, my mother sent me next door to the nuns to attend their kindergarten. It was immensely convenient; I ducked through a gap in the privet hedge and managed to arrive at my place in line (we were sized by height) before the bell had stilled. Moreover, I felt very much at home in the convent, as I had been a frequent guest on Sundays after Mass, when the sisters enjoyed a lovely brunch. The mother superior of the order, Mother Rosarine, spoiled me outrageously—I heard this repeated at home, almost daily—and I usually sat on her lap at the table. Because the public school was a mile away (this was before the era of yellow buses), my attendance continued at the convent through second grade, at which time the crucifixion of Jesus became as much an issue for me as animal cruelty. No matter that I was told on our side of the hedge that the Romans had done that to Him. On the other side, quite matter-of-factly and without casting blame on my innocent state, it was the Jews who had fastened Him to the Cross. A larger-than-life-size crucifix hung in the main corridor of the schoolroom; daily there was no escaping this piteous sight.

The Jesuits are reputed to say, "Give us a child until he is eight and he will be ours always." I was deeply touched by my early experience at convent school, but the final effect of my bifurcated religious education was quite simply to feed my skepticism. Jesus became for me a symbol of goodness and humility that I never quite relinquished, a very human figure in an otherwise mysterious faith full of saints available for special intercessions.

The year I moved to public school, my middle brother Herbert came down with a virulent case of pneumonia that did not respond to any of the usual treatments. A pair of nuns from next door came every day at sundown to pray at his bedside until daybreak. Meanwhile, the doctor, in desperation, prescribed a new medication called sulfanilamide that was just coming into use in Europe and North America. Herbert made a rapid recovery, whether due to science or divine intervention.

Despite the presence of the sisters in their long

black gowns and starchy white wimples, Germantown then was largely an upper-middle-class Protestant suburb. Several Jewish families, even some not related to us, had also invaded the precinct.

To be a Jewish child in Germantown in the thirties was sometimes difficult. On bad days, older kids chased us downhill from school yelling *Christ-killer!* In class, a schoolmate might mutter *I don't want to sit next to a Jew.* Among adults there was an omnipresent but invisible line that divided Jews from non-Jew-hating Christians. Both of my parents spoke with pride of their "good Christian friends." But it was clear that this level of friendship differed from friendships within the brotherhood. There were things they didn't say in front of "the Gentiles." There were in-group jokes, sprinkled with yiddishisms, which could only be told in the right company, and there were tacit admissions of abhorrent traits. My mother, for example, was driven wild by any of us gesticulating in the course of a conversation. "Don't talk with your hands!" she hissed. "You look like an immigrant." Until I was in my teens I believed that only Jews used gestures or stood close enough to breathe on each other as they conversed.

My earliest visions of my mother place her in an

evening dress, about to depart in a cloud of French perfume for an important social event—a gala evening at the symphony under Stokowski's baton, the opening performance of a stage play featuring Katharine Cornell or the Lunts, or some anniversary party. She wore an evening cape of black velvet, its full length sprinkled with what looked like multicolored nonpareils. As she swept out the door, I was suffused with longing to look in on what it was the grown-ups did on these occasions. I knew they drank foamy concoctions called Brandy Alexanders or Grasshoppers, for I had tasted these and found them unbelievably bitter. What kept them out so late? I remember how hard it was to fall asleep until the parents, those Olympians, were once again safely under the same roof as we. And after the Lindbergh kidnapping in 1932, when my father had iron bars installed on my bedroom window overlooking the porch roof, sleep was even more elusive.

"Early to bed and early to rise," my father used to say with a wink, "and you never see any of the regular guys." Nevertheless, he was up at dawn every day except Sunday. He worked long hours, pausing only for a milkshake at noon, never returning home before 6:30 p.m. Monday through Friday. On Saturdays the store stayed open until 10:00 p.m. Sometimes, my mother and I would drive to South Philadelphia to meet my father as the store was closing and the heavy metal guard gates were being locked. We then drove to a section of the city known as Strawberry Mansion, where, in my father's favorite delicatessen, we enjoyed a midnight supper of whitefish, sturgeon, Swiss cheese, and half-sour pickles. Outside, on warm spring evenings, an old man wearing a yarmulke sat on an upturned keg and played his violin in the minor key. I was told he played to usher out the Sabbath.

These were the only glimpses I ever caught of the pawnshop world that provided for the capacious house in Germantown. My mother, I began to understand, was racked with ambivalent feelings. Of proud German-Jewish origins, she felt she had married beneath herself. Because my father was a descendant of Russian Jews, hers virtually constituted a mixed marriage. Her mother-in-law still kept a kosher house except when the grandchildren came to visit and milk magically appeared on the table next to the meat. She still spoke Yiddish, a forbidden tongue in our upwardly mobile household, although my father insouciantly peppered his speech with Yiddish expressions.

My mother was clearly uncomfortable with my father's profession because of its Shylockian stereotype and she hid it in conversations with strangers by referring to him as a "broker" or "merchant." I grew up exposed to the stereotype of pawnbrokers as hardhearted and greedy Jews exploiting the working-class poor who relied on them as a way to get quick cash. Cartoons showed a man with big hands, black hair, and a hooked nose that invited the viewer to draw his own conclusions. Later on, when I was old enough to fill out applications that asked for "father's occupation," I was brought up short. My mother told me simply to write "broker," but I had lived with her ambivalence long enough to share it; I understood that the one word would doubtless be read as "stockbroker."

These dichotomies pursued me into adolescence, and I think my experience was not atypical for American Jews of my generation. Parents made great efforts to assimilate into the suburban culture, but only up to a point. They went to their own country clubs, they organized their own dancing classes for their offspring (and these, in my circle, were further stratified into most desirable, less, and least, a hierarchy based on elusive criteria of social standing). Parents did not approve of mixed dating, which led to mixed marriages, but they desperately wanted their sons and daughters to go to Ivy League or Seven Sisters colleges, where they were most easily enticed away from their parochial views.

Hardest of all, there were gradations of Jews. We were expected to observe these as rigorously as we observed certain behavior when in the company of Christians. These injunctions were laid down by my mother, who was extremely conscious of origins and income. In the case of, for example, the de Sola Mendeses, who were descended from Sephardic Jews (this term in its earlier version referred to Spanish Jews who came to the New World before the American Revolution) and were, in my mother's euphemism, "not well-off," origins canceled out income. The Mendes family was not only acceptable but sought-after company. In the case of (here I will invent a name) the Glitskis, who owned a department store chain and lived garishly in a mansion, income overrode origins and they too were written into the canon. But the vast land between these two examples was pocked with pitfalls: nouveau riche who were too nouveau for polite society, Sunday school classmates whose residence in West Philadelphia indicated their families were recent arrivals, and so on.

Philadelphia Jewish society, it seems to me at this safe remove, was as intricately structured and as frail as the towers my brother Peter built with his Erector set.

Named Edward Elias on his birth certificate, he refused to answer to any name but Peter when he started public school, on grounds that "I look like my daddy and I sound like my daddy and my real name is Peter." Jewish children are not named for the living, whether out of superstition or religious dictum, but Edward Elias's name was legally changed when he turned six.

While many of the children in our neighborhood were sent off to Germantown Academy, Friends Central, or Penn Charter, all four of us attended public schools. My father did not approve of private school education; it did not prepare you to meet the real world. In many ways he was fiercely plebeian, proud of his humble beginnings, his decision to leave school early (he finished high school by attending night classes) while his older brother stayed on. I suspect it was not need but restlessness that impelled my father to drop out of school. An autodidact, he was something of a mathematical wizard. He used to astonish us children by doing enormous sums in his head. He could multiply and divide, carry decimals into six places, split percentages into splinters without benefit of pencil and paper.

My three brothers all graduated from rough-and-tumble Germantown High School; I was spared. My mother prevailed on my father to accept her ingenious compromise. For $200 a year I could attend public school out of the district in Elkins Park, a very upscale community with a far superior school system and a wealthy Jewish population. Here, I repeated eighth grade, which helped close the age gap that had resulted from skipping two years in grammar school. I was lucky to slip into the last year of the experimental Columbia University eight-year study group, where students advanced at their own pace retaining the same teachers through the various curricula. Dutifully I plodded through algebra and plane geometry, but in Latin and English classes my soul leapt up.

I have written elsewhere about Juanita Mae Downes and Dorothy Lambert, two heroic figures who made a profound difference in my life. With Miss Downes I studied Latin year by year, moving from Caesar's *Gallic Wars* through Cicero to Virgil (including the forbidden Book IV set in Dido's cave; Miss Downes was a purist and omitted nothing). My senior year in high school was largely devoted to translating stories from Ovid's *Meta-morphoses* into matching hexameters. In Mrs. Lambert's English class, I read all of Dostoevsky and, for ballast perhaps, Hopkins, Arnold, Housman, and Hardy. This wonderful teacher believed as devoutly in the rules of prosody as any of my nuns had believed in the Second Coming. Once again, I was an enthusiastic convert and could scan the metrics of any poem as well as deduce its form—sonnet, pantoum, villanelle, etc.—by the time I graduated.

Commuting to and from Elkins Park was hazardous, an hour in the morning by trolley, then racing to catch the train; an hour and a half in the late afternoon via the same route but with longer waits between connections. Once I turned sixteen and had acquired my driver's license, my mother allowed me to take her car one or two days a week, a much appreciated boon as by then I was one of the editors of the weekly high school *Cheltonian* and needed to stay late on Thursdays to put the paper to bed. But I started school in Elkins Park as an outsider and ended as one, respected yet friendless in a social structure that yawned above me. The fathers of my classmates were doctors, lawyers, academicians, the owners of department stores or drugstore chains. I was a pawnbroker's daughter. There was no room for me in the established cliques. I had two friends: a polio-paraplegic boy who was the sports editor of the weekly paper and a black girl who played the violin and was subject to epileptic seizures. I ate lunch alone in the locker room or in the girls' toilet, sitting in a locked cubicle with my legs pulled up out of sight. Eventually I was accepted at the far end of a table in the lunchroom but seldom invited to take part in the conversation, which circled around parties beyond my reach.

The passage through adolescence was a lonely, introverted time. Forced to attend dancing class on alternate Saturday nights, where all of the popular girls were indifferent students in my French or history section, I hid in the ladies' room until the ordeal ended. I took refuge in scholarship; getting all A's was my only balm.

My Aunt Bea—my father's sister-in-law and my mother's archrival—began to take an interest in me as I emerged into adolescence. She gave me her own set of Louisa May Alcott novels. Until then, I had read only *Little Men*, *Little Women*, and *Jo's Boys*. Still awaiting me were her dog-eared copies of *An Old-Fashioned Girl*, *Eight Cousins*, and *Rose in Bloom*. Little by little she fed my romantic nature with Edna St. Vincent Millay and

Elinor Wylie, Willa Cather, and Ellen Glasgow. The mother of two sons, she was lonely for a daughter. My mother, who was, I thought, fiercely critical of me for not conforming to her standards of femininity or social grace and for failing to worm my way into the Elkins Park clique, was nevertheless reluctant to share me.

But I was not the prime battleground between these two strong-minded women. Aunt Bea fancied herself a linguist. She had spent several years in Paris during a period when her mother had made a disastrous second marriage, and she was of course fluent in German, for her mother had been born in Berlin. Moreover, Aunt Bea had a college degree and many of her friends were educated women. My mother had left the conservatory at nineteen in order to marry my father. She had grown up in a small town among chickens and cows, not cathedrals and museums. Although she had won an elocution prize for reciting "The Curfew Shall Not Ring Tonight," although she had played the organ for the Methodist church every Sunday, she had not sojourned in Paris nor set foot in the Louvre. And while she maintained a lavish table and raised abundant bright flowers, her bookcases did not wrap around the living room crammed with alphabetized authors, many of whom had signed their volumes. This undeclared vendetta sustained these women well into their old age.

I remained in the vortex of the little tempest they generated. Each time I returned to Germantown from college, I reentered Aunt Bea's cloister like a celebrity. She mixed and served, in place of tea, a Dubonnet-and-gin concoction that was sweet enough to drink and powerful enough to induce giddiness. My mother so fulminated against these visits that, twenty-five years later, when each of them was widowed and lived a few blocks apart in central Philadelphia, I had to resort to considerable subterfuge to continue to see my aunt even briefly. It was a terribly sad ending; little by little she grew senile and toward the end recognized no one. I think even my mother, who longed for revenge against her lifelong adversary, was shocked by this ignominy.

During childhood and adolescence all of us siblings attended Sunday school at Temple Rodeph Shalom, a Reform synagogue in Philadelphia. Here we received a double message. We were exhorted to be proud of our Jewish heritage but enjoined savagely from Zionism. We were not in favor of planting trees in (then) Palestine. As late as 1940, we were required to write an essay titled "America, Not Palestine, My National Homeland."

Reform Jews in that congregation did not learn Hebrew beyond the alphabet and a few simple prayers. These were taught by rote; there was no effort to treat Hebrew as another language with its own grammar. Pronunciation was still old-style Ashkenazi, referring to the Jews of France, Germany, and East Europe. There were no chuppahs, no yarmulkes, certainly no stamping on glasses at weddings, which we were told was a leftover paganism. The services at Rodeph Shalom were almost indistinguishable from Unitarian services—we even sang some of the same hymns.

At Camp Watitoh in the Berkshires, where I spent July and August from the age of eleven until the summer I was married, Friday night services were held in an outdoor amphitheater where candlelight combined with the strong aroma of citronella to create the appropriate ambience. Campers were encouraged to write their own liturgy. Here I fell out of the bosom of the Almighty into the strong arms of pantheism. I wrote reams of purple prose in praise of the oversoul, although I did not know that far more systematic thinkers had preceded me. It was here that, along with the oversoul, I developed proficiency as a swimmer, moving up from the American Red Cross–certified beginner to advanced swimmer and on to water safety instructor. This eventually earned me status as head of the camp's waterfront, a paying job that came with my very own Social Security number.

The Mendes family members who owned Watitoh were Sephardic Jews (old-style Sephardic) and ardent Zionists. I felt as though I were in the enemy camp, where coins were collected to plant the very trees in Palestine that our Philadelphia rabbi had so vigorously opposed. As my skepticism grew, Jesus looked more and more temperate to me by contrast.

It wasn't just the Zionist issue. I didn't know much about the Spanish Civil War, but I knew we sided with the Loyalists. The rise of Nazism in the thirties colored all our lives. My father had always been a newshound. Now he followed the Fascist acquisitions of the Sudetenland and Czechoslovakia with worried interest. The America Firsters outraged him. Neville Chamberlain was a traitor. As the dreadful truths began leaking out of Nazi Germany, my father received a spate of letters from relatives, or relatives of relatives, in Poland, begging for his assistance to emigrate. One of my most vivid memories from this period is of coming upon my powerful parent, uncharacteristically seated at the dining room table long after the dishes had been cleared away, with crumpled pages of a letter spread before him. His head was in his hands and when he looked up at me, I saw that he was in tears. It was a wordless moment, but I understood. Finally he spoke. "They will all die," he said. "This is the pogrom to end all pogroms."

For long before it was public information, news of the concentration camps had sifted into the Jewish community. No one else seemed to care. Even my father's beloved Roosevelt failed him. I began having horrendous nightmares of being pursued and captured by the Nazis, just as after the Lindbergh kidnapping I had had nightmares of pursuit and capture by the mailman, who stuffed me into his mail sack and carted me away. A deep sense of guilt for having been born a safe American Jew haunted me. By an accident of fate I was to survive while millions went to labor camps—we did not quite know about the ovens yet. In sympathy with my father, I began to share his news broadcasts. I was educated in the root causes and outbreak of World War II by such radio commentators as Raymond Gram Swing, H. V. Kaltenborn, Elmer Davis, Max Lerner, and Fulton Lewis Jr., who boomed into our living room, telling the same tale over and over, but from divergent viewpoints.

Although we were not devout, we did light candles every Friday night and say the Sabbath blessing in our house. We celebrated Hanukkah by lighting the eight candles of the old brass menorah supposedly carried across the Atlantic by my great-grandfather, we ate homemade hamentashen at Purim, and we held enormous Passover Seders—one night only, of course—attended by all of my mother's family within reach, as well as by my father's brother, with his wife and two sons, two sets of courtesy aunts and uncles, and an occasional stray, someone stranded in Philadelphia over the holiday. It was a family practice always to include one or two "good Christian friends" to celebrate Passover with us. Somehow I felt we were actors performing a famous play for their edification.

Not that we were deprived of Christmas. For many years we had a tree, somewhat hidden from view, on the upstairs landing, complete with winking lights, tinsel, and ornaments. We children got presents, as did the cook and her husband. But our Christmas was a private, almost shamefaced celebration informed by the sneaking sense that we had no right to it. We lived in a Christian world; we were in it, if not of it. Unfortunately, we were not exactly "of" the world in which we did belong.

In addition to my growing discomfort over my father's occupation, our well-to-do lifestyle made me uneasy. To supplement the married couple who served as our live-in cook and butler/chauffeur/handyman, the once-a-week laundress, and the weekly gardener, my mother hired a "governess" to look after my brother Peter and me, although she was not called by that title. A young German girl who had immigrated to the States in 1920, she came to live with us a few years before I was born. My mother addressed her as Agnes, other adults, Fräulein, but we four children called her Froy. She shared my room, sleeping in the other twin bed until I was six years old, when she left to marry a German restaurateur. We stayed in touch faithfully. After I was married, I continued to visit her. My husband Victor and I took the children—the youngest was still in arms—to see her in Haddon Heights, New Jersey. Even though it was almost lunchtime, she lavished ice cream and cookies on them. I was quite taken aback by her permissiveness, for I had remembered her as kind, but strict.

Nothing in my childhood surpassed my love for Froy. She was truly my mother. Her departure left a deep wound that was almost unbearable for many years; somehow I had become convinced that she had gone away because of a flaw in my character. My mother, who had little patience with children and a busy social life of her own, reinforced this notion by exclaiming at least once a day that I had "changed" since Froy departed.

I lost my ability to speak German almost instantly, although it had been my mother tongue. I lost completely the considerable vocabulary I had had, and over a lifetime I have never regained it. Froy's brother had served on a U-boat in the First World War. Her parents still lived in Bremen. With the news coming from the Fatherland in the early thirties, it was hard not to think dark thoughts of being rejected by her. And what about her husband? Someone with the same last name was a member of the German-American Bund. These and other rumors swirled around my head. Years later, I learned how painful this period had been for Froy and her family.

Froy, Aunt Bea, my two remarkable high school teachers, Mother Rosarine, and my own mother all played a significant part in my gradual maturation. Now college loomed. Although I had applied to Wellesley, which not only had a fine swimming pool but also an underwater observation room for analyzing swim strokes, I was not accepted. For while they did not openly practice the quota system, virtually all the top colleges and universities at that time—1942—sharply limited the number of Jews and other minorities they accepted. Instead, I attended Radcliffe, which I confess I had never even considered until being rejected by Wellesley. The Cliffie basement pool wasn't even regulation-size. In high school I had swum weekly for the Women's Athletic Association and been invited to join Billy Rose's Aquacade, a cavalcade of synchronized swimmers who were going to Chicago, Minneapolis, and points westward to perform. They would be paid $100 a week and chaperoned at all times. At seventeen I was still a minor. Of course my father refused to give me the permission required.

At Radcliffe, I swam for the team all four years and captained it in my senior year. I also stood lifeguard duty over the lunch hour—the pay was a dollar a day— and taught swimming to those few students who had somehow never mastered the rudiments. One could not receive a diploma in those days without passing a simple swimming test in deep water. Cliffies were denied access to the Harvard pool even for their swim meets until the 1970s.

At Radcliffe, epithets with which I had been

branded—bookworm, greasy grind, brain trust—now became a badge of honor. Dorm life brought me into contact with girls from vastly different backgrounds and geographies. Hemmed in by rigid parietals, we quite easily fell into the pattern of late-night bull sessions in the smoking room. (Virtually everybody smoked.) Politics, the war, our sex lives, our post-grad aspirations came under scrutiny. And boys; although they called us girls, we came to call them men. Cambridge was full of uniforms. The navy was turning out ensigns at the business school; they were known as ninety-day wonders. The army had language training programs in Russian and Chinese at Harvard. Because of the war, Cliffies no longer had to attend separate classes, but were finally integrated into the regular lectures in Harvard Yard. But not the libraries. Widener was open to women; Houghton was not.

At Radcliffe my life began anew. My parochial Jewishness fell away. Unselfconsciously, I found friends of varying beliefs and hues, some in the camaraderie of the swimming team and the freshman crew, my new sports enthusiasm, others through proximity in the dorm, and still others in the course of developing a social conscience.

In 1943, the Fore River shipyard workers went out on strike in an effort to vote in a union of their own. With a few other Cliffies, most of them juniors and seniors, I rose at dawn, caught the 6:00 a.m. subway to Ashmont, where an antique station wagon belonging to the CIO met us, and reached the factory gates in time for us to hand out leaflets as the round-the-clock shift changed. Later, after breakfast in a diner (my first diner!), we helped with the writing and layout of the union newspaper, a weekly. My high school experience with layout served me well. I became the chief headline composer and wrote much of the dialogue of *Ralph the Foreman*, a satirical comic strip.

I did not report this new activity in my weekly letters home; some uncharacteristic caution caused me to withhold my enthusiasm, even though my father was a Democrat and believed firmly in the New Deal. To my astonishment I received a furious phone call from him. My father had never before initiated such contact. He demanded that I stay away from Fore River and give up all union activities. The FBI had taken out a dossier on me. An agent had paid my father a personal call alerting him. The union effort, he said, was being marshaled by Commies and fellow travelers and now I had a record linking me to these dangerous Reds. My parent threatened to take me out of school if I didn't comply. I countered by saying I would get a scholarship and join a work-study plan and stay. The argument ended in a draw.

Where did the courage to defy my father come from? Looking back, I can only see it as part of my coming of age. None of this, I later gloated, would have happened had I been accepted at Wellesley with its underwater observation room. Nor would I have met on a blind date the army sergeant and Harvard graduate I was to marry sixty-six years ago.

II.

Love in Wartime

Maxine and Victor in front of the club for noncommissioned officers in Amarillo, Texas, 1945. *Kumin Family Photo*

For half a century referred to in the family as the long-lost love letters, they were only recently discovered in the most predictable location—the farmhouse attic, snugged under several abandoned picture frames that formed a false bottom in an old metal camp trunk. Remarkably, thanks to their insulated incarceration, they survived in fragile but still legible condition—575 letters exchanged between Cabot Hall, Cambridge, Massachusetts, where I was a junior at Radcliffe College, and P.O. Box 180, Santa Fe, New Mexico, where Victor, a Harvard graduate, was a sergeant in the U.S. Army. The Santa Fe address was a fiction, one that the top brass worked hard to preserve; Victor was actually stationed on "The Hill," as it was locally known, at the Los Alamos Laboratory, where he was one of the soldier-scientists working to develop the atomic bomb.

We met on Patriots' Day, April 19, 1945, on a blind date. During the five remaining days of Victor's furlough, there was no war. We did not speak of FDR, one week dead. We did not know that V-E Day lay two and a half weeks ahead. We walked for miles along the Charles River. We went to the zoo. We went to the ballet. Evenings we repaired to a booth in the dark fastness of the Hotel Lafayette bar, nursing drinks until my curfew loomed: ten o'clock on weekdays, midnight on weekends. Was this called falling in love in less than one week? Or was this Marvell's "vegetable love" that would "grow vaster than empires, and more slow"? We had months and months to find out.

In his first letter, Victor described his heroic route back to New Mexico—one train from Boston to St. Louis, another to Kansas City, a third to Pueblo, Colorado, followed by a bus to Santa Fe: *"The Road Back" was not nearly as unpleasant as I had expected but for a four-hour stretch of standing on my head (it was the only way I could fit into the car). . . . The bus trip from Pueblo to Santa Fe . . . was nothing less than overpowering. As we rode easily down from Las Vegas to Santa Fe the metamorphosis from day to night took place painlessly as the brilliant sunset faded. And then the mountains, particularly "Starvation Peak," standing erect in all their war-like glory. There was so much beauty that only a poet or a painter could capture it—the pueblo huts, the farms, and most of all the native Mexican Indians, people living life on their doorsteps and in their huts lit by kerosene lamps.*

He is careful not to mention the last leg of the journey, a 36-mile climb up to Los Alamos, set 7,000 feet above sea level on a high desert plateau. Once it had been a boys' boarding school, a site laboratory director J. Robert Oppenheimer had chosen for its seclusion. Now it housed the labs, machine shops, barracks, and dining facilities that had transformed the mesa into a bustling town of 8,000 people.

On May 8, the war in Europe ended. I wrote the following to Victor: *At 12:30 today a sea of white-capped officers and WAVES and army boys stood at attention in the Yard facing the steps of Mem[orial] chapel and the student body and good citizens of Cambridge stood on the steps of Widener.* [Dean Willard] *Sperry* [of Harvard Divinity School] *was at his simple best and altho it always strikes me that there is something incongruous in hearing the words of an unknown Deity echo hollowly thru a scientific apparatus known as a loudspeaker, it was a fine thing to hear these hundreds and hundreds of people sing their national anthem, while the choir on the chapel steps with their crimson and black robes flapping in the breeze made themselves heard over all the rest. Long sentences always seem to get the better of me, don't they? Especially today, I think, because I was really so impressed. There was a color guard of Old Glory and the Harvard crest and sailors with guns—and high over University Hall three magnificent huge flags are flying—the stars and stripes, the unionjack, and . . . the hammer and sickle. Yup, the red flag high in Harvard Yard. There was a bright spring sun and the lawns had been freshly cut, the Yard a huge mass of people full of a warm relief, if not elation, the chapel bells and the organ music . . . we were rather carried away with it all. People seemed to be less jubilant than thoughtful, tho, knowing we are only halfway thru the job.*

His rather doleful reply presents a sharp contrast: *Thanks for the wee bit of godliness. V-E day was celebrated here in the same spirit, but a different manner. Free beer and sandwiches; a little guzzling, a movie, to bed. And so I honored the end of the European war.*

Our early letters cautiously skirted mention of the intimacy that had begun to develop between us. We set about exploring half a dozen schemes to see each other again as soon as possible. A trip to Little Rock, where my oldest brother was stationed, after serving in the North African and Italian campaigns, seemed feasible. I would keep his wife company and help with the new baby (I knew nothing about babies). I concocted a trip to Amarillo, Texas, where my newly divorced uncle was a captain in the army and his daughter, Bobby, my girl-hood chum, was a dental technician. The price exacted for the train ticket to Amarillo, bought by my reluctant parents, was for me to spend two weeks in Little Rock on baby duty afterward.

June 11: *I asked Bobby to wire me about reservations in Amarillo; if the fates are kind, I'll arrive there on Wednesday the 27th and leave there for Little Rock the following Monday. If I don't sound too excited about it, the fault is all Oscar's* [my typewriter] *because he's all tuckered out from typing a 30-page paper on imagery in Henry James and so you mustn't expect too many !!!s from him. The enthusiasm is all ours, Vic, but I must admit that mine is very tempered with a weight of responsibility . . . which amounts in my befuddled brain to being "mature and sensible." . . . I'll be on pins and needles until I hear from you definitely. I guess I just can't believe that our plans are working out, and that may account for my sobriety. It seems too good to be true that we'll see each other again in just about two more weeks.*

Victor is almost as somber: *This will probably be the last letter you'll receive before I leave, if all goes well. Since I cannot fly without priority and priority is limited to officers, it means a twelve-hour bus trip which should get me to Amarillo 7:00 A.M. Thursday, June 28. The inevitable return must begin at noon Sunday. . . . And so, pursuing my normal routine of reveille, inspection, retreat I try to speed the burning of the days left before I see you. The bad feature of this, of course, is that the process of combustion will accelerate beginning June 27th and almost before it has begun, my 3-day pass will be over.*

Only a few hours after I settled into Bobby's apartment, a Western Union telegram was delivered, dated 7:02 p.m., June 27: "PASS SCHEDULE SCRAMBLED ARRIVE MIDNIGHT TONIGHT WILL TRY TO REACH YOU STAY AWAKE VIC."

Neither of us remembers the moment of our reunion, although I am certain either Bobby or my uncle shepherded me to the bus terminal. I know that we spent the rest of the night in separate quarters. I was assigned the pullout couch in my cousin's living room, and Victor was shunted elsewhere.

It was 105 degrees in Amarillo the next day. My uncle lent us his car and we spent several hours in an air-conditioned cinema, making out in the back row. When we exited, Victor had forgotten where he had parked the car. I remembered only that it was green. It took us half an hour to find it.

The day before Victor was to return, my uncle, on his own initiative, used his connections to reserve a pre-paid hotel room for us in Albuquerque. Perhaps the fact that he was cohabitating with an army WAC elicited his sympathy for the lovelorn pair. We were surprised and grateful; the distance Victor had to travel back to Santa Fe would be narrowed, thus extending his leave. We took a late-night bus, which broke down in the desert. While the driver spent an hour with his head under the vehicle's hood, the passengers all disembarked to enjoy the cool air. There was a gibbous moon. The cactus roses were in bloom. Twenty-four hours of privacy in Albuquerque ensued.

We both wrote to each other on July 2. Victor had seen me off an hour before his bus was scheduled to leave. My letter begins, *Although I only left you some hours ago, it seems much longer and Alby and the weekend far away. . . . [T]his is not the way to start a letter to you, sweet, telling you that I miss you and I love you—but just wait. I'll think of something else to say yet.*

His letter is just as lovesick: *To have seen you cry was the greatest thrill of my life . . . one of the things I shall never forget. . . . And now the everlasting struggle, the gnawing wait. . . . I'd like to be completely senseless for eight months. But since that's impossible, I'll conjure you up wherever I go. The pleasure of seeing you in every tree, in every cloud and every mountainside—that will have to keep me sane.*

I was home in Philadelphia with my parents, struggling to get through the several weeks before I could return to Cabot Hall, when the news broke. August 7: *Well, the most exciting news of the war—and of all time— broke today: the atomic bomb. We've been glued to the radio since 5 o/c when we first got news of it. Somehow the idea of harnessing the atom is almost too big to get around in a single thought—and it carries a lot of sobering thoughts with it. Obviously the nation that was first to discover the secret is the conqueror; and along with the confident thought that the war with Japan is now just about a fait accompli comes the tremendous realization that man has finally discovered how to destroy civilization. I don't know if the comprehension of this will be the necessary restraining influence on a world armed to the teeth—on a world that suddenly awakens to a vast new knowledge that will revolutionize warfare. . . . I have that "Milton, thou shouldst be living at this hour" feeling. . . . What a horrible world this is when mass extermination comes to be spoken of so calmly and with such calculation.*

A powerful moment of dramatic irony here—I obviously had no idea that Victor's "doing something technical" in Santa Fe involved him in the development and detonation of the atomic bomb.

Victor, the same day: *One ear is still glued to the radio speaker. Over and over I've heard it. . . . This is it, and my emotions vacillate between ecstasy and real nausea. . . . My uncle's three words, <u>war is obscene</u>, apply more than ever. And this, though it is the crowning achievement not only of the past year's trials but also of much of the time I spent at Woods Hole, makes me sick. Here I am, wallowing in the success of the most daring experiment ever attempted and the most important development in the history of civilized man. What it all means politically, economically, morally is earthshaking. . . . The successful mastering of the technique for releasing atomic energy (fission) can make life on earth vastly better—or it can destroy it. . . . I am naively proud to have contributed to it. July 16 was the first test—made here on the New Mexico desert at Alamagordo—and we stayed*

*up all night to await the flash which was supposed to be
visible in a radius of one hundred miles. News of its success
made us want to write to everyone too soon but we were still
bound to secrecy. We knew it would be only weeks before the
launching over Japan.*

But there was more. One day later: *Dr. Oppenheimer
thanked the men of the Special Engineering Detachment*
[to which Victor belonged], *making it clear to everyone
that detonating the bomb could not have been accomplished
without their assistance.... For half an hour he spoke on the
moral aspect of the discovery—of his intense hope these past
months that the Japanese would surrender before the bomb
could be dropped ... that America is now using this awful
weapon was decided by the highest men in government ...
that the necessity for using it makes the cruelty of it no less
sickening, that the thought of killing perhaps a quarter of a
million people in one blow rests heavily on his soul. He also
stressed that possession of the fundamentals belonged to no
one group of men. Such talk renews my faith in humanity.
... You're now free to tell anyone where I am and what
I've been working on and also to discuss anything that is
revealed publicly.*

This was the first time I had heard of Woods Hole,
or the circuitous path that led from Victor's graduation

in 1943 to Los Alamos in September 1944. Initially he planned to volunteer for the Naval Air Corps before he could be drafted into the army, but E. Bright Wilson Jr., the professor of physical chemistry who had been his adviser at Harvard, discouraged him. Wilson asked, would you rather be a dead hero or make a significant contribution to the war effort? He offered Victor a chance to join his group at the Oceanographic Institute on Cape Cod, where he was the director of the Woods Hole Underwater Explosions Lab.

Victor rented a room in a retired fisherman's house. He and the other bachelors on the staff ate in an old Dutchland Farms ice cream shop, where their meals were prepared. At some point, three of his colleagues disappeared overnight, their living quarters mysteriously vacated. A steady stream of visitors from the navy and elsewhere came to follow the program's evolution. George Kistiakowsky, a Harvard physics professor, dropped in several times to consult with Wilson. They discussed the progress of Victor's underwater detonation experiments.

And then in June 1944, the hammer fell. Even though Wilson and other Woods Hole higher-ups tried to get him deferred, Victor's draft board was determined to meet its quota. He was summarily drafted into the army and sent on June 6, the day of the cross-Channel invasion by the Allies, to Fort Devens, Massachusetts. From there he was shipped to Alabama for basic training in the infantry. After sixteen weeks of up to 25-mile marches with a 20-pound pack, he was called back from final field maneuvers, given a train ticket to Santa Fe, ordered not to talk about his destination to anyone en route, and on arrival to call a local telephone number from a specific public telephone booth.

Victor never knew who ordered him plucked from the infantry and reassigned to Los Alamos, but when he met them on The Hill the morning after he arrived, he felt certain it was his two Harvard professors, Wilson and Kistiakowsky. A few days later, he encountered the colleagues who had gone missing from Woods Hole.

I don't know when I found out these details, certainly not until the war was over. Whatever Victor was doing in Santa Fe, he couldn't talk about it. He couldn't talk about the male civilian, a putative German spy, who visited the Woods Hole facility and went from room to room chatting with lab personnel. Or that a chain-link fence went up overnight and a guard was posted at the only entrance to the institute the next day. He couldn't talk about the person who sidled up to him at the Harvey House restaurant stopovers en route to Santa Fe, each time asking, "Hey, soldier. Where ya going?" He never knew whether he was being tested by the brass or spied on by a Nazi.

On August 9, Victor continued his dramatic commentary: *The second atomic bomb has been dropped. Nagasaki is shrouded in a death-pall of smoke. We wishfully expect the surrender to be announced momentarily but honestly we expect it will take from 30 days to six months.*

Unfortunately, I failed to date most of my letters beyond assigning them the days of the week. Here is part of my response to the news: *I am so glad that you're not a secret anymore, or at least only technical details are secrets. I almost turned into an india rubber ball on Monday when the news story broke and Santa Fe and Los Alamos made the front page, and somehow, probably irrationally, I am as proud of your part in this greatest discovery in history as if it had been your brain child alone. Your philosophical discussion of its implications is so superior to anything I might attempt to say now that I will avoid redundancy. . . . The Potsdam agreements are I think rational and sensible. Of course tampering with national boundaries cannot help but create irredentism, but we are faced with an impossible alternative. As for Truman: Certainly not a dynamic speech, certainly not an orator, but there is a quiet sort of confidence in his voice and his way of stumbling over polysyllabic words has I think a greater appeal to his "common man" than FDR's magnetism. FDR is sorely missed.*

The terms of the Japanese armistice were announced on August 15. The next day, Victor's letter began, *This is the second of a two-day drunk for most of the outfit. Monday night was a terror what with smashing up the recreation hall, leaving all the water faucets on, stripteasing in no less secluded a place than the middle of the street. . . . The radio says that Oppy is in Washington, and rumor hath it that he will buck for our discharges. No real news about that yet.*

Mine of the same day: *We'd been glued to the radio the entire day. . . . That the second world war is over is still not easy to believe, but our immediate reaction was pretty close to tears. The personal element means so much to this family* [my three brothers had all served overseas] . . . *it's hard for me to grasp what the cease fire order means on a dozen battlefronts. I think today of what heartbreak there must be in those homes where peace will not bring back the dead and victory bells ring hollowly. . . . I'm skeptical that we haven't won a permanent peace . . . reconversion will be painful and chaotic and so many of our boys will come* *home to unemployment and inflation and bitterness. . . . I'm wondering what will happen to Los Alamos now that the war is over. The duration obviously won't <u>durate</u> for several months. . . . Releasing members of the armed forces is going to be slow, but if they'd just station you on this coast. . . . I know, dream on.*

Daily exchanges about possible dates of discharge, even of actual furlough in November, followed. This disconsolate excerpt from Victor is dated August 22: *Prospects of discharge within the next year look very remote. Nothing is definite and won't be for 3 months, but we have every reason to expect a royal raw deal leading perhaps to basic training all over again and God knows what else. . . . Meanwhile there is November to think about and that's soft solace to my soul.*

My reply by return mail is an effort to reduce the gloom: *Nine weeks is just nothing; it's weeks, it's not even months, and weeks shrink so much more perceptibly than months. It only takes a few days to make a dent in a week, whereas it takes weeks to make a dent in a month. Nine little weeks, then it will be November and it will be you. . . . Darling, I'm not incoherent, am I?*

There were substantive issues as well. On the same day, this exchange, first from Victor: *World events seem to be leading to a precipice, but not as fast as national ones. Truman is probably bucking for Term II but he's gonna have a big problem on his hands come the mad scramble for raw materials, franchises, jobs, and discharges. The Wagner-Murray Bill* [the Wagner-Murray-Dingell bill was never enacted] *cannot in itself create full employment. . . . A plan for orderly reconversion is the necessary prelude. . . . Only a strong economic planning commission with authority to decide and power to enforce remedial measures could handle the enormous problems caused by Truman's political maneuvers.*

And this from me: *The abrupt shutting off of Lend-Lease is a very discordant note. I could cheerfully throttle every big-businessman who sings the "why should we be Santa Claus" tune, and willingly orates from a soapbox to every misguided man in shirtsleeves who listens unwittingly to Wall Street wail. God, if we do the same stupid things after this war that we did after the other—reparation in gold, high tariffs, wildcat financing—well, turn from that and take a look at the state of unpreparedness we're in for reconversion.*

Our letters continually crossed in the mail. On September 17, Victor wrote enthusiastically about Henry Wallace, FDR's two-term secretary of agriculture, then his third-term vice president: *Wallace's "Sixty Million Jobs," particularly his remarks on the budget and the "fuller life for all," have removed all doubt in my mind of his ability to become a great president. . . . I could quote for days the things that have endeared him to me—on the function of the federal government in stimulating private investment, on the necessity of planning the elimination of the business cycle without jeopardizing the freedom of initiative . . . on education as the basis of maintaining (or creating) political and economic democracy, the "fundamental decency of man." . . . This is a man who has successfully embedded a practical course of action in a living philosophy.*

My letter on the same day: *Every day that things look a little grimmer I doubt . . . that capitalism can do the job. I am afraid of state socialism but I think that it is like being afraid of the dark, in that they are both inevitable. And I am infinitely more afraid of depression, unemployment, despondency and class war than I am of national socialistic economic planning.*

A day later: *Days are always nice when there's a letter from you because no matter how brief or commonplace you apologize for their being (god wot grammar) they are always different and every day I learn something new, something that makes me think I either know you a little better or else that, my god, he is a complete stranger to me. I wonder if you ever get that feeling. Here we are struggling gamely to hang onto our ties to one another and to build on them and I think it is a tribute . . . to our high school English teachers that we have managed so well this far. You know, people generally do not do this—they write to each other, yes, and they are in love too, but they don't pick up subjects and interests and dissect them and discuss them and tease them out day after day.*

The contrast between our daily lives sharpened when I returned to Cabot Hall. I was immersed in an atmosphere of warm collegiality. Victor was grinding out day after day in a barracks shared with fifty-nine other disgruntled soldiers as impatient as he. September 18: *Final word: we are to stay here until we acquire the necessary number of points or years of service under the discharge plan as applied to the army as a whole. We'll get no special consideration—and no more than one point a month . . . and so we go on sweating out endless days of morbid monotony and bitter boredom.*

Victor's two-week furlough—minus two days' travel in each direction—was hectic and rewarding. We traveled from Boston to Philadelphia to announce our engagement. Victor, pro forma, asked my father for my hand. A brief dialogue ensued: "What would you do if

I said no?" "I guess I'd just marry her anyway." "In that case, I say yes." A bottle of champagne was brought out, previously chilled. Victor borrowed money from his brother-in-law for a ring.

Back in Los Alamos on November 28, Victor wrote, *As this day wore on, I realized I am chained again and all the mountains have enclosed me in a sea of apathy, bitterness and longing. . . . I am once again a soldier. I will do this and I will do that—all because we have a new post commander who bulges with West Point protocol.*

Two days later, censorship was lifted. All my letters to Victor until then had arrived resealed with a tape that read "OPENED BY U S ARMY EXAMINER." The face of the envelope bore a stamp that read "PASSED." We had written freely back and forth discussing Marxist theory, the Soviet Union, the labor union movement. I was a fierce advocate for the CIO, ever since I leafleted for its adoption at the Fore River Shipyard during my freshman year, and an FBI agent visited my father.

Nevertheless, nothing in our Cabot Hall–Santa Fe letters was redacted by the individual who scanned them. We were not on a watch list at that time. After he left Los Alamos, Victor told me this true spy story: each morning, walking through the tech area to pick up supplies for the day's field operation, his group would see David Greenglass (brother-in-law of the ill-fated spy Julius Rosenberg) working on a lathe fabricating molds for casting the explosive lenses. When assembled, these components would form a hollow sphere, which would contain plutonium, the heart of the fission bomb. One of Victor's colleagues always taunted him as they passed, calling, "Hey, Greenglass! Whaddya know?" Greenglass, who knew quite a lot, never acknowledged their presence.

(After Victor's discharge, the FBI tracked us none too subtly for about three years, calling on our neighbors and paying me direct visits while Victor was at work. Soon thereafter, Greenglass was arrested and accused of spying for the Soviet Union in 1950. We never learned whether the surveillance was carried out on all G.I.s in the Special Engineering Detachment of which Greenglass had been a member or whether we had been specially selected.)

On December 6, I wrote, *Reading the morning Times these days is painful and worrisome—our policy in China, corruption in Korea, a lot of stupid people up in arms and ready to fight Russia tomorrow, Asiatic nationalism busting out all over, anti-labor legislation on Truman's desk, an uninformed public ready to sanction a race in atomic armament. . . . Right on down to the inside page where the AMA is blasting the proposed national health insurance program. . . . I wonder if, when you crawl into bed at night, your mind turns eastward as mine does westward. You are with me always in a hundred different ways.*

We began subversively planning ten days in Santa Fe, where I would stay in "anything better than a Y" and work on my thesis. I even made tentative plane reservations; Victor's brother-in-law had offered to lend me the fare. It would be reading period, which meant I would have to miss only two classes. Victor could come down The Hill for two weekends.

On December 13, my bad news: *I met with Prof. [Elliott] Perkins this morning and discovered to my surprise that the thesis is UPON ME. . . . Due at typist Feb. 28th. Tutor wants to see first draft Jan. 3. Preposterous. Got it moved ahead to the 10th. Still preposterous . . . I have made a start and will be at it hammer and tong every minute from now till then. I am going home from the 20th to the 26th and then must come back, bury myself in isolation at St. John's* [dormitory of Harvard Divinity School] *and will try hard. If it is physically possible he'll get his damn draft. . . . But Santa Fe, my darling, I can't come. . . . Somehow I will get thru until May without you and I feel much worse for the disappointment it will be to you than I do for myself. I at least have Cambridge and the good life to keep me going, and you don't even have that.*

A hiatus in letters occurred between December 18 and January 10. The Los Alamos facility's water lines, which had been laid aboveground, froze during an unexpectedly protracted cold snap. A deep well was dug in the valley 7,000 feet below the lab, and milk trucks were contracted to bring enough water up to The Hill to maintain essential services. Since the truck engines were burning out at a prohibitive rate along the steep incline, the decision was taken to drastically reduce the number of personnel until water flow could be restored. Victor was one of the lucky soldiers selected to receive an extra furlough.

It was Christmas week. The war was over. Service members were being discharged, whole families were on the move. Congestion on the railroads was overwhelming. Passengers packed the aisles; some climbed into the overhead baggage racks. Soldiers raided the dining car on boarding; there was no food available en route. Victor managed to buy sandwiches and Cokes through the coach window when they stopped at stations along the way. He traveled east for three days, standing for much of that time, finally arriving at my parents' house at 4:00 a.m. on December 22, unwashed, unshaven, and very hungry. He must have telegraphed at some point along the way because I knew he was coming, but not when.

We returned to Cambridge the day after Christmas, I took up residence in the dorm at the Divinity School, and Victor laid out the following schedule. I was to work on my thesis every day from nine to five. He would arrive punctually at five, and we would go out for dinner and be together until midnight. The bar at the Lafayette Hotel continued to serve as our hangout. This rigorous arrangement worked well. By the time Victor departed on January 9, I had a draft of the pretentiously titled "Amorality and the Protagonist in the Novels of Stendhal and Dostoyevsky" and went on under the guidance of my tutor, Harry Levin, to complete it.

The hazards of rail travel continued. On January 10 Victor wrote from the railroad station in St. Louis: *Arrived here four hours late . . . encountered a wreck in Ohio, got rerouted thru Alabama, (!) missed the streamliner to Colorado . . . waiting now for the 11:50 to Kansas City . . . should hit Santa Fe 11 a.m. Saturday. Just means signing in 12 hours late, risking k.p.*

The next day he continued his saga: *Hopped the cattle car in Kansas City—sat with a pilot over a leaking steam line—nabbed a porter who got us a little deal up front in a chair car . . . we shared eats and seats and sweated out the tortuous ride together. . . . The barracks, as expected, is still bursting with inane invective. Work conditions are apparently the same. . . . There is a plan in operation whereby men can be discharged to take jobs here under contract till June 31st.*

Although it sounded tempting, Victor rejected this option. He was determined not to participate in stockpiling atomic weaponry. Initially, his group went out on the mesa each day to a site where it had worked on lens explosions and played touch football instead. A new group leader, a former naval officer, threatened to have him court-martialed for this. Nothing came of the threat. Ultimately, Victor was reassigned to the procurement department and given routine clerking duties.

The remaining months inched past on The Hill. Sometimes Victor was able to procure a typewriter, one that desperately needed a new ribbon, but the news was unchanging—discharge not likely before he had completed his twenty-four months of service.

In Cambridge, I underwent orals, examined by

professors Michael Karpovich, Crane Brinton, and Harry Levin.

No words, darling, could recreate for you the diabolical horror. . . . It was a very refined torture. The victim was allowed to cross her legs and smoke cigarettes and even blow her nose should she feel so inclined. . . . Every time I said yes I should have said no and conversely. . . . When Levin asked me what Turgenev and Tolstoy quarreled about, I smiled sweetly and asked, did they quarrel? Thereupon my magna flew out the window. Historical fact: Tolstoy challenged Turgenev to a duel over their religious differences but later apologized.

Just before departing, Victor wrote, *This is the last letter I will write to Cabot Hall . . . unless some twenty years hence we have a daughter of our own going through what you have just finished . . . and you are visiting her.*

On June 5 I graduated cum laude from Radcliffe College. The next day, my twenty-first birthday, Victor was discharged. We were married in Philadelphia on June 29.

Two weeks later, we moved into a barely furnished apartment in Woods Hole in the old U.S. Bureau of Fisheries building. At night, seals barked outside our bedroom window. Every other morning the iceman came with a fresh block for our wooden icebox. Meat was still rationed but we dined on flounder we caught off the wharf. Mussels and clams were abundantly available. Victor came home for lunch every day from the Oceanographic Institute, fifty yards away. We never wrote to each other again.

Maxine and Victor at a nightclub
in Boston, 1945. *Kumin Family Photo*

III.

Metamorphosis: From Light Verse to the Poetry of Witness

Maxine at her desk in Newton, Massachusetts, late 1950s. *Carl Chiarenza*

How did I become a very old poet, and a polemicist at that? In *The Writer's Chronicle* of December 2010 I described myself as largely self-educated. In an era before creative writing classes became a staple of the college curriculum, I was "piecemeal poetry literate"—in love with Gerard Manley Hopkins and A. E. Housman, an omnivorous reader across the centuries of John Donne and George Herbert, Randall Jarrell and T. S. Eliot. I wrote at least a hundred lugubrious romantic poems. One, I remember, began:

> Lonely on an August night I lie
> Wide-eyed beneath the mysteries of space

And watch unnumbered pricks of dew-starred sky
Silent drop past the earth with quiet grace . . .

Deep down I longed to be one of the tribe but I had
no sense of how to go about gaining entry. I had already
achieved fame in the narrow confines of my family for
little ditties celebrating birthdays and other occasions,
but I did not find this satisfying. There were no MFAs
in poetry that I knew of except for the famous Iowa
Writers' Workshop, founded in 1936; certainly there was
nothing accessible to a mother of two, pregnant with her
third child in 1953 in Newton, Massachusetts. I have
noted elsewhere that I chafed against the domesticity in
which I found myself. I had a good marriage and our two
little girls were joyous elements in it. But my discontent
was palpable; I did not yet know that a quiet revolution
in thinking was taking place. Of course motherhood was
not enough. Perhaps I could become a literary critic?

Hoping to find direction, I subscribed to *The Writer*,
a Boston magazine. There I found my destiny in an
advertisement for Richard Armour's *Writing Light Verse*,
$3.95. I would begin there and if I hadn't published
anything by the time this baby was born, I would turn

my back on the Muse forever. My first-ever four-liner appeared in *The Christian Science Monitor* in March of that year. When the check for five dollars came, I had recovered my investment in Armour's book, and had broken into print with this:

> There never grows so red the rose,
> So sound the round tomato
> As March's catalogues disclose
> And yearly I fall prey to.

I had been ghostwriting articles for some local doctors on subjects ranging from the benefits of electroshock to the treatment of third-degree burns, spending Saturdays at a medical library in Boston while Victor took over my domestic role. Now I had found a profession that was infinitely portable. I could try out lines in my head while doing the dishes or hanging the laundry—no dishwasher, no dryer—or conveying a child to a music lesson or the dentist. I grew adept at composing in the car while I waited for the musician or patient to be trained or treated. Here is one I've dredged up from my memory bank:

People who sleep like a baby
Don't mean what they say. Or maybe
They have no scions who wake
At midnight with ill-defined ache.
Nor have they at 2 yet another
child bringing her nightmare to Mother.
No indeed. If they had, they would gather
That this simile is mere blather.
As for me, I am happy to own up
I would much rather sleep like a grown-up.

Before long, I was being published in the pages of
The Wall Street Journal and the *New York Herald Tribune*,
and I was frequently appearing in *The Christian Science
Monitor*. I also won acceptance in the *Ladies' Home Journal* and *The Saturday Evening Post*, among the leading
magazines of the time. "Lines on a Half-Painted House"
appeared in the *Post* in 1955:

In summer, beach and billows beckon;
And in between, you dab a speck on.

In autumn, who feels dutiful?
The foliage is beautiful.

In winter, little can be done;
The brush will freeze, the nose will run.

Spring's the time! The perfect instant!
And fortunately, two months distant.

About these lines I must add this incredible detail: Victor, as my husband, was required to provide a letter from his employer certifying that my poem was original. This is not as far-fetched as it sounds today. In the fifties, women, along with people of color, were still thought to be intellectually inferior, mere appendages in the world of belles lettres.

Writing light verse actually served me well as a poet. It pressed me into the exactitude of rhyme, and working in rhyme allowed me to trot some of my dark poems out of the closet and try to cast them in formal patterns. I greatly admired Edna St. Vincent Millay's sonnets, especially her skillful Petrarchan ones, all but unmatched to this day; W. H. Auden's deft tetrameter also pointed me forward.

I continued to write in isolation until 1957, when I stumbled upon a poetry workshop at the Boston Center for Adult Education conducted by the poet and Tufts

University professor John Holmes. Anne Sexton and I met in that class; our deep personal and professional relationship ensued and ran for seventeen years until she took her own life. Holmes became my mentor, and in private I called him my Christian academic daddy. He proposed me for membership in the New England Poetry Club and soon thereafter put me up for my first academic position at his university.

Still, entry into this circle of emerging poets only highlighted the tension I felt at having to juggle domestic and professional spheres. This acrobatic act dominates a letter I wrote to my mother in 1958 to wish her a belated happy birthday:

> Just call me Mrs. Pepys. Up sooner than
> betimes; dryer broken, youngest out of
> underpants. All underpants soaking wet
> on line. Pouring. Ten minutes of earnest
> persuasion, no one would know he was
> wearing old baby pair, no one would
> see. Find plastic bag to protect violin
> case. (Pouring harder.) Write check
> for violin teacher. Overdrawn? Live
> dangerously; payday Wednesday. Find

cough drops for middle child. Middle
child coughs anyhow. Girls depart.
Youngest watching Captain Kangaroo.
Make beds, do dishes, get dressed; car
pool late for youngest, writer late for
appointment. Car pool comes, writer
leaves; rushes to Tufts. Interview with
chairman of English Department, 30
minutes. Consults my resume. What
was Slavic course you took junior year?
Think back; possibly 19th century
Russian history. Discuss elements of
English renaissance? Writer knows little
about this period. Bluff. Next meet
chairman, Freshman English. Amiable.
Each have a cigarette. Back to chair
of department. Accompany him across
campus (still pouring) to meet Dean.
Dean looks too young to shave. Has five
children. Further discussion. Money not
mentioned. Interview over. Decision
after June 16. Arrive home, gobble
sandwich, deliver girls back to school.
Go pick up youngest, rush to bank for

cash. Overdrawn? Live dangerously. At
bank, youngest's stomach feels squirmy.
Suspicious green tint to complexion.
Throw up? Abandon plan to go to
market. Rush home. No temperature.
Does not throw up. Borrow neighbor
in case; go to market. Husband's sales
director coming for dinner. Husband
has clean shirt? Whiskey sours? No rye.
Can't find noodle pudding recipe. Find
it. Make pudding. Girl Scout cookout
postponed, rain. Stops raining. Clean
chicken, set table. Middle child comes
home. Cello case? Lost. Found. Deliver
middle child and cello to lesson. Home.
Toss salad. Start children's dinner.
Retrieve child and cello from lesson.
Poets from workshop call, farewell party
for John Holmes Friday night? Bake
cake? Tomorrow. Find children for early
supper. Throw on dress; husband and
sales director arrive. Drinks. Dinner.
Children to bed. Guest leaves and so
betimes to bed.

I remember that life well. I was just beginning to get my "true" poems published, first in little magazines like *Audience* and the *Beloit Poetry Journal*, then acceptances from *The Atlantic*, *Harper's*, even *The New Yorker*. I remember teaching freshman comp part-time to phys ed majors and dental technicians; I was the first woman ever hired in the Tufts University English department and therefore not to be trusted with liberal arts students.

Coming of age as a poet in the late 1950s and well into the '60s, I was not unconscious of the disdain with which aspiring women poets—and people of color—were treated. Gradually I came to realize how arduous the road to acceptance as a woman artist would be. Attitudes changed at a glacial pace. I have cited elsewhere, more than once, an event that took place in 1967. At a dinner hosted by the Poetry Society of America, Robert Lowell rose to praise Marianne Moore as the nation's best *woman* poet. Blessedly, Langston Hughes leapt up to assert that she was the best *Negro woman* poet in the country. What astonishes me is how few women today, hearing this story, appreciate the irony in it. Was she black? they ask.

In 1961, when my first book appeared, it was one of forty-odd poetry collections published in the United

States that year. Just eight were by women. (That statistic and the following ones are provided by Wikipedia.) By 2011, the major trade publishers, independent presses, university presses, online publishers, even self-publish presses, had engorged that number and Wikipedia no longer listed them all, instead posting only the eighty-some poets chosen for David Lehman's annual *Best American Poetry* anthology. By my rough count, thirty-plus were women. This year (2012), Bill Henderson's Pushcart anthology processed approximately eight thousand poems that had been nominated for a prize by contributing editors and assorted journals. It seems safe to say that poetry, in all its permutations from rap lyrics to *sonnets redoublés*, is flourishing.

Holding one's first published collection of poems is matched only by the thrill of holding one's newborn child for the first time. I could hardly believe my good fortune. In 1961, the same year that *Halfway* came out, the Radcliffe Institute for Independent Study announced the recipients of its largesse. Incredibly, both Anne Sexton and I were among the twenty-four women who received grants in fields ranging from poetry and painting to science, history, and philosophy. Although the dollar amounts were small, the grants authenticated us. They said we were real and what we did was valuable.

The Radcliffe Institute's validation freed me to see myself as a writer. Although poetry was my first and remains my most enduring love, I wrote extensively in other genres. I never felt any ambivalence about working in prose; in a comforting way it relieved the tension of the high-wire act of writing the poem. When my children were small I turned to writing stories for them, many in tight rhyme. Richard Wilbur, Jarrell, and Eliot had sanctified this terrain before me, and I found it joyful and relaxing. Now, only a handful of my twenty-five children's books remain in print; all five novels, my first memoir, and my one collection of short stories are out of print; as far as I can tell, my four essay collections are still available.

In the mid-sixties, John Ciardi, director of the Bread Loaf Writers' Conference in Middlebury, Vermont, offered me a coveted position as a fellow. I declined, citing some bogus reason; the truth was I was too scared to accept. The prospect of rubbing elbows with a faculty of prominent writers paralyzed me. Luckily, Ciardi persevered. In 1969, when he invited me to join the Bread Loaf staff, I screwed up my courage and agreed. The experience was exhilarating, the atmosphere relaxed and friendly. I went back five more times.

When my fourth poetry book, *Up Country: Poems of New England*, won the Pulitzer Prize in 1973, I was stunned. The news came in a phone call from a local television station; I was certain someone was perpetrating a cruel hoax. Once I was persuaded the award was real, I was aghast. Harper & Row were, too. In six weeks they managed to renew the print run and bring out a paperback edition as well. However, when my editor, accompanying me to my first reading at the 92nd Street Y in New York, announced cheerfully, "This should be fun. I've never been to a poetry reading before," I was so unsettled that I misplaced the carefully annotated list of poems I planned to read and had to choose as I went along.

That summer after the flurry of interviews, including appearances on TV, I fled from suburban Boston to our derelict former dairy farm in New Hampshire. Candide's advice to cultivate my garden helped center me. I was truly afraid I would never write again—but the poems came, as they always had, on their own terms, beginning in the most unexpected ways and demanding that I pay attention. What was also unexpected was the flow of invitations to give readings and teach at a wide array of colleges and universities. Before the Pulitzer, the only major invitation I had received was thanks to Howard Nemerov, who had recommended me to Centre College as visiting professor. Danville, Kentucky, was a venue more exotic than Paris or Rome would have been. After the Pulitzer, I was an adjunct professor at Columbia. Next came two Fannie Hurst Professorships in succession at Brandeis University in Waltham, Massachusetts, and Washington University in St. Louis.

The following year we sold our snug little Cape Cod colonial in Newton, Massachusetts, and moved to New Hampshire full-time. To my surprise and frequent consternation, I was launched in the poetry business; PoBiz Farm became the name of the craggy, hilly, overgrown property we were bent on restoring, and where we had started to raise horses. I was a wage-earning poet and an amateur distance rider. Often, flying to gigs in faraway states, I took my lightweight synthetic saddle with me in its own case. When someone next to me at the baggage claim asked, "What's in there?" I replied, "A tuba." En route to various outposts in California or Missouri my seatmate invariably asked me, "What do you do?" I never said that I was a poet because experience had taught me the rejoinder would be, "That so? Ever published anything?" I learned to say, "We raise horses," which was true and ate up much of my income.

Poetry and horses, with long days of labor (some of it hired but mostly our own) to reclaim cow pastures from the second-growth forest, dig postholes and put up wooden fences, sand and repair or replace ancient clapboards. Along with the sprucing up, the books of poems accrued, a new one every three to four years. I left Harper & Row for Viking in 1975—who needed an editor who had never been to a poetry reading?—and then left Viking after the decision was made in 1989 to use the photo of a glossy Bambi-like fawn on the cover of *Nurture* instead of what I had lobbied for: a tiny kangaroo joey held against the immense scale of a human hand.

W. W. Norton became my publisher and Carol Houck Smith my editor. We did eight books together, one of them a collection of essays and stories, and each graced by a Wolf Kahn painting. I remember with particular fondness the afternoon we spent with a manuscript spread out on the double bed of my cramped room in the old Gramercy Park Hotel as we bumped our way around deciding which poems went with which others.

Then Carol said, "Shall we go see Wolfie?" and we made our way several blocks uptown to the gallery and chose one of his glorious landscapes. Once I had been a suburban matron. Now I had lived so long in the country that I was skittish walking in the rush-hour crowds of pedestrians and crossing streets where impatient taxi drivers honked and gestured. Diminutive Carol asked, "Would you like me to hold your hand?" Looking down at her, I said, "Yes, please."

I was never comfortable in New York City; the canyons between skyscrapers felt ominous. By contrast, Washington, D.C., with its height limit on buildings, seemed airier, greener, less hectic. As the newly appointed 1981–82 Poetry Consultant to the Library of Congress (a position renamed Poet Laureate four years later), I was able to select several women poets to read in a monthly series. Best known among them was Adrienne Rich, who had rejected previous requests from male laureates; that day, the line for admittance to the auditorium stretched around the block. I also instituted weekly brown-bag lunches in the august Poetry Room, little used except for formally welcoming foreign poets. If my tenure is to be remembered for anything, let it be for those Thursday lunches where well-known writers brought their students or disciples for a noon gathering that often stretched to 4:00 p.m.

In 1995 I was appointed a chancellor of the Academy of American Poets alongside Carolyn Kizer. Together we lobbied for the appointment of the black poet Lucille Clifton to fill a vacant post, but twice we saw the vacancies go to white males. In November of 1998 we resigned in protest, which ultimately led to the restructuring of the board: no longer could chancellors serve two consecutive twelve-year terms, and women and minorities achieved representation. We were praised by many and damned by a Procrustean few.

Over the years many of my poems were rooted in the rural landscape; this led to my receiving the jocular epithet Roberta Frost. I didn't disavow this, but I did feel that it marginalized my work. Still, when Denise Levertov, a poet I admired for her lyric voice, began to write fierce poems against the escalating involvement of American troops in Vietnam, I had worried that her polemic would somehow damage her extraordinary gift. (It did not.)

Looking back, I see that as early as 1971 I confronted ethical issues in my own poetry. In "Heaven as Anus" from that year, a poem attacked as pornographic

by a major public figure, I seized on the U.S. government's use of animals for experimentation. It opens:

> In the Defense Department there is a shop
> where scientists sew the eyelids of rabbits open
> lest they blink in the scorch of a nuclear drop

and closes with these lines:

> It all ends at the hole. No words may enter
> the house of excrement. We will meet there
> as the sphincter of the good Lord opens wide
> and He takes us all inside.

In 1982, in "Lines Written in the Library of Congress
after the Cleanth Brooks Lecture," I wrote about the
relationship between poetry and history:

> Poetry
> makes nothing happen.
> It survives
> in the valley of its saying.
> Auden taught us that.
>
> . . .

New poets will lie on their backs
listening in the valley
making nothing happen
overhearing history
history time
personal identity
inching toward Armageddon.

For much of my poetic lifetime, my focus was on the natural world, untampered with and unromanticized. But the face of violence and human cruelty eventually broke through—perhaps abetted by the fact that I have a daughter who worked for thirty-two years for the United Nations refugee agency. Hence my anguished rant against the Bosnian war and its impact on civilians in the 1994 sonnet "Cross-Country Skiing," which doesn't abandon the natural world, but puts it in perspective:

I love to be lured under the outstretched wings
of hemlocks heavily snowed upon, the promise
of haven they hold seductively out of the wind
beckoning me to stoop under, tilt my face

to the brashest bits that sift through. Sequestered,
I think how in the grainy videos
of refugees, snow thick as flaking plaster
falls on their razed villages. Snow
forms a cunning scrim through which the ill-clad
bent under bundles of bedding and children appear
nicely muted, trudging slow motion to provide
a generic version of misery and terror
for those who may step out of their skis to sit
under hemlock wings in all-American quiet.

In the same vein, "Mulching" talks of reading the head-
lines while spreading old newspapers between plants in
the vegetable garden:

. . .

prostrate before old suicide bombings, starvation,
AIDS, earthquakes, the unforeseen tsunami,
front-page photographs of lines of people

with everything they own heaped on their heads,
the rich assortment of birds trilling on all
sides of my forest garden, the exhortations

of commencement speakers at local colleges,
the first torture revelations under my palms
and I a helpless citizen of a country

I used to love. . . .

My disenchantment turned to fury as the war in Iraq gathered steam, with the appalling use of torture by the United States and its proxies, the legal maneuvering at Guantánamo, and more. Now, nearly sixty years after my first four lines of light verse were published in *The Christian Science Monitor*, I feel that my work has truly metamorphosed into the poetry of witness, though my political poems were wrung from me. Some, like "Red Tape and Kangaroo Courts," are in unrhymed sonnet form. One, "Entering Houses at Night," evolved as a villanelle; another, "What You Do," as a pantoum. Thematically, these poems are linked by my despair at the monstrous contempt American officialdom has displayed for justice and morality in the years since the 9/11 attacks:

and the list of things that are prohibited
in the camps is itself prohibited

. . .

and capital cases are heard with no
capital defense attorneys allowed
  (from "Red Tape and Kangaroo Courts I")

. . .

We went in punching kicking yelling out orders
in our language, not theirs.
  (from "Entering Houses at Night")

. . .

when you shackle them higher
are you still Christian
when you kill by crucifixion
  (from "What You Do")

Although metrics serve as a way of giving shape
to my anger and enabling my poetry to voice moral
outrage, some of my rants are in free verse. Whatever
methods writers in all genres use, we have to bear witness, hew to our personal compass, and stand up to be
counted. To paraphrase Auden in his prescient poem
"September 1, 1939," all we have is a voice "to undo the
folded lie." Today we have literally thousands of poets

raising their anguished voices, not just in English, but in Arabic, Russian, Farsi, and a hundred other tongues. Are our poems succinct, stunning, intensely moving? Of course we hope they are. Do they change the course of elections, undo death penalties, pardon political prisoners, expose fraud and corruption? These are rhetorical questions, but the poetry of witness at least provides a living archive, exposing the folded lies.

IV.

Our Farm, My Inspiration

Maxine and Victor Kumin, 1976. *Georgia Litwack*

Mornings, from my desk, I have a clear view of the paddock and, beyond it, the first of five intersecting fields. Every morning, finding them empty comes as a fresh surprise. The grass is green. No horses graze. No dogs are busily sniffing to check what may have passed through in the night. Along the stone wall that leads uphill to our farmhouse the daffodils are in full bloom. Above the farmhouse our ambitious vegetable garden is restarting. The pond that replaced a marsh gives back the reflection of white pines that encircle it. We have grown old here. My husband, Victor, is ninety-two, and I recently turned eighty-eight. All six of our rescued dogs are gone. Our alpha mare lived to an ancient thirty-five. Eight foals were born and raised in our hand-built stable. This is the world we came to as flatlanders, where we found good neighbors and where we grew to be true New Englanders.

In 1961 we were restless parents living in a modest Cape Cod cottage on a handkerchief-size lot in Newton, Massachusetts, a Boston suburb. Caught up in the demands of three kids, ages thirteen, eleven, and eight, what we needed was some sort of country retreat not more than a two-hour drive away. And then $10,000 dropped into our laps. Half of it was passed down to me in an inheritance from my grandmother. Almost simultaneously the other half came to Victor when his mother died. On a drizzly fall Saturday, we drove up to see a real estate agent in New Hampshire, and the search began.

My mother was appalled. Why, she demanded, did we want to sequester ourselves from the vibrant social and intellectual life greater Boston offered? What was wrong with us?

I couldn't tell her how I felt. The words stuck in my throat. Even if we had had the income to sustain it, I desperately did not want my mother's life. Nor was I satisfied with my suburban life of teaching two English composition classes part-time, chauffeuring the children to and from the dentist, to their lessons on violin, cello, and clarinet, and dealing with day-to-day hazards of house-keeping. The lost socks, the white blouse that has turned pink from proximity to a never-before-washed red sweat-shirt. The missing dog leash, followed by the errant dog. And the endless Saturday night dinner parties where wives outdid one another with inventive hors d'oeuvres and cocktails of grenadine and pineapple juice. I could have been a case study from Betty Friedan's *The Feminine Mystique*, not to be published for two more years.

On the surface my mother looked content with her role as wife and mother, a queen of leisure, but I knew she had once aspired to a career as a pianist. As I wrote in a poem called "Life's Work," she told me she had been "at eighteen a Bach specialist / in a starched shirtwaist / begging permission to go on tour / with [a] nimble violinist . . . and my grandfather / . . . saying no daughter of mine . . ." had forced her to abandon her dream. The following year she eloped with my father. I understand why I had to have the white-gown nuptial complete with Lohengrin's Wedding March. I am still struggling to understand why she wasn't more sympa-thetic to my own ambition at that time.

I was trying to become a serious female poet in a male-dominated field. The reigning poets were T. S.

Eliot, W. H. Auden, Randall Jarrell, Marianne Moore, and Elizabeth Bishop, not a mother among them. None writing lines like these from "Nightmare":

> This dwelt in me who does not know me now,
> Where in her labyrinth I cannot follow,
> Advance to be recognized, displace her terror;
> I hold my heartbeat on my lap and cannot
>   comfort her.
>
> . . .
>
> The first cell that divided separates us.

My first book, *Halfway*, had been published in a print run of 1,000. Three hundred copies would be sold. The rest would eventually be pulped. A first book was all too often a first and last. I needed space to be able to get on with my declared vocation. Victor was holding down a demanding job as a consulting engineer with a Boston firm, and he too needed quiet space between the Monday-through-Friday pressures. He shared my restiveness with the social expectations of our suburban life, the weekends of enforced exchanges with other couples with whom we had little in common. While stationed in the mountains of New Mexico during the war, he had learned to ski. He looked forward to finding a base for returning to this sport and introducing our kids to it. The youngsters themselves saw a weekend hideaway as an exciting place to bring friends. We needed to find a little cabin in the country. Possibly with a brook. Possibly with a sunny patch for growing our own tomatoes. Without neighbors, no matter how kindly, who could see into our windows on either side.

My father, who had always also been a flatlander, was equable. He cautioned us only not to buy land on a hill. I didn't remonstrate; I knew that New Hampshire was full of hills, but I let the matter drop. That fall the real estate agent patiently drove us up hills and down dales. A house on a pleasant pond was surrounded by other houses. One beside a brook abutted a gravel pit where trucks churned in and out. A charming cottage on the outskirts of a town felt, well, too suburban. After the first snowfall we suspended our search.

The following spring we resumed the hunt for what Victor had begun to call the Hope Diamond. We rejected two more possibilities before the agent turned off the state road, swung through our first-ever covered bridge onto a dirt road, and after a mile made a right-hand turn onto another that appeared to be barely one car wide. "I don't have a key to this place but you can look around and see what you think," he said. My neck hairs were rising.

The road curved steeply uphill for almost half a mile, then came to a dead end between an old white farmhouse and a massive barn with a haymow. The house roof was missing many shingles. Half of the massive barn sagged in on itself. Before we opened the car doors I knew we had found our diamond.

To look into the farmhouse windows, we had to fight our way through a dense growth of blackberry brambles. Tree saplings warred with a thick stand of lilacs that sprawled along the stone wall separating the road from what had once been a front lawn. The back of the house looked out on forest in all directions. The downhill side of the barn opened onto a barren patch that might have been a turnout area for livestock. Behind the tumbled-in back end of the barn the remains of a small stony pasture were visible. I suddenly realized there were no other houses on this nameless road. No sound of vehicles in the distance. No voices. The silence filled with bird calls.

I didn't know it just then, but this poem, "Country House," was brewing. It opens:

> After a long presence of people,
> after the emptying out,
> the laying bare,
> the walls break into conversation.
> Their little hairlines ripple
> and an old smile
> crosses the chimney's face.

We came back the next day with the agent and a key. The property, known locally as the Old Harriman Place, had stood empty for six years. An artist and his wife from New York owned it. They had divorced and were anxious to sell. Several dead birds and more than several dead mice lay scattered about. The birds, the agent told us, had probably flown down the two chimneys. Field mice, he shrugged, were part of country living. He suggested a cat was in order. Yes, it had running water, fed by an underground pipe from a well behind the house. Two woodstoves were the sole heating source. Victor, ever the engineer, headed for the cellar, agent in tow. Meanwhile, I scouted the layout of the rooms.

All the wide-board floors had been painted dark red. A broad wainscoting that ran along two sides of the living room was painted a creamy white. The kitchen contained a sink and an ancient stove. A small lavatory was tucked behind the kitchen. Wide boards framed the hall vertically all the way up to the second-floor ceiling. They too had been painted off-white. Three bedrooms opened off the upstairs hall, as did a serviceable bathroom. There was a tub but no shower. Serviceable enough, I thought. I knew the house was old but I didn't appreciate its antiquity at that point. What was inside held little interest; what attracted, even thrilled me was the landscape, the huge shagbark hickory trees, the forests of white pine and hemlock, ragged bits of open land surrounded by birch saplings. We were in a different world, one, it now seemed, I had always been looking for.

Arrangements were made to bring a civil engineer colleague of Victor's to look the house over. The asking price was $13,000 but we could make an offer. How much land came with the house and barn? A hundred and twenty-five acres, more or less. (The acreage turned out to be considerably less, but we were able to augment it over the years.) The house dated back to 1800. Miles of stone walls dotted the woods, evidence of what had once been sheep pastures. The cavernous second-story haymow and remnants of leather halters suggested an era of dairy farming had succeeded the sheep. A little one-room structure had probably been used as a spring-house to keep the milk cans cool.

That summer we made an offer. The owners made a counteroffer. There was another round between the art-ist, now living in Mexico, and our agent. It was early fall before the Old Harriman Place, RFD 1, Joppa Dis-trict, became ours for $11,500. We began to come and go weekends all through the winter, as further described in "Country House":

> . . . Field mice coast down
> a forgotten can of bacon fat.
> Two clocks tick themselves witless.
> October, clutching its blankets,
> sidles from room to room
> where the exhausted doors
> now speak to their stops,
> four scrubbed stones of common quartz.
>
> . . .

They are gone,

those hearty moderns who came in

with their plastic cups and spoons

. . .

torn between making over

and making do.

At their leavetaking

the thin beds exhale.

The toilet bowl blinks,

its eye full of purple antifreeze.

We started learning bits of its history. The spring-house, commonly placed over a natural spring or creek, was vital because electricity had not come up the hill until the end of World War II. The well that fed the house was a shallow, hand-dug hole. After the papers were signed, the agent took Victor aside. "You'll need to have a proper well installed first thing," he said. I am happy that he was wrong. Fed by a spring that spurts from a crevice in the rock at the very bottom, the well has withstood periods of drought that dried up our neighbor's—yes, we had one neighbor half a mile away. Elderly, loquacious, he had lived there all his life, working at the local sawmill.

On the first day he came calling, he stooped down and handed me an odd pointed object. It was my first porcupine quill. I had no inkling of the hundreds of these I would encounter, the needy dogs we would take in, and the vet bills we would accrue for quill removal.

Henry was destined to become the fictional hero of my numerous Henry Manley poems, beginning with the following excerpt from "Hello, Hello Henry":

My neighbor in the country, Henry Manley,
with a washpot warming on his woodstove,
with a heifer and two goats and yearly chickens,
has outlasted Stalin, Roosevelt and Churchill
but something's stirring in him in his dotage.

Last fall he dug a hole and moved his privy
and a year ago in April reamed his well out.
When the county sent a truck and poles and cable,
his daddy ran the linemen off with birdshot
and swore he'd die by oil lamp, and did.

. . .

. . . Henry
walked up two miles, shy as a girl come calling,

Maxine Kumin

to tell me he has a phone now, 264, ring two.
It rang one time last week—wrong number.
He'd be pleased if one day I would think to call him.

Hello, hello Henry? Is that you?

He remembered well the old dairy farm. Times the
cows got loose and he helped round them up. Times
the farmer was short-handed and he helped with the
early-morning milking. He explained that the big
three-storied barn, built into the side of the hill to take
advantage of the slope, also provided shelter from the
wind. What would many years later become a walk-in
horse barn with six stalls had served as the pit for cow
manure. He pointed out the trough, now boarded over,
through which the dung had been shoveled. The second
story once held a season's worth of fodder. Before this
space was eventually reincarnated as an apartment in
1976, we found stacks of homemade picture frames and
several muddied oil paintings. Our artist predecessor
had held painting classes there at one time.

Henry told us the porch that ran across the front
of the house had been glassed-in during the 1930s.
Later, we would dismantle half of it to allow the sun to

brighten the pine-paneled dark living room. Invited to tour the house, our sage of yesteryear told us that the wide-board floors were pine and could be sanded down if we didn't like the red paint. Red was a traditional color for floors and the outsides of barns because it wore well. The living room wainscoting was also pine, king pine, according to Henry, although he couldn't account for the name. (A little research revealed that in 1761 King George had claimed sole rights to all pine trees in the New World that exceeded twenty-four inches in diameter. This dimension was later revised downward to twelve inches, a restriction that came to play a part in the outcry, "Taxation without representation is tyranny.") Henry pointed out that the wide vertical boards on the walls in the hall had been hand-planed. Peering closely, we could see uneven striations left by the tool. These boards too could be stripped back, a herculean task undertaken fifteen years later. In the attic we inspected the roof beams, whole chestnut-tree trunks, some still with bark on them. One beam was mysteriously notched in groups of fives. Henry suggested this was a way of keeping count of something stored here, something that wouldn't be harmed by freezing. Possibly butternuts, a popular winter treat when he was a boy. Sadly, the butternut trees—also known as white walnut—were dying off, victims of a fatal canker, as the chestnuts had before them.

That first fall, we acquired the habit of leaving Newton as soon as the Friday supper dishes were cleared away. Our dog Caesar positioned himself in the front hall where our bags were piled, making sure he wouldn't be left behind. Stalwart campers, we settled into the unheated farmhouse on spare mattresses. Living conditions were spartan, but that didn't matter. There was so much to explore. We found half a dozen cellar holes along the rangeway that once climbed above our house all the way to the next town. It had been a stagecoach road with kiss-me-quicks, level places to halt the team and allow the horses to catch their collective breath. Now the way was barely wide enough for humans to pick along in single file. Stunted apple trees grew close by some of the cellar holes. Where the forest canopy permitted, several of the early settlements displayed stands of lilacs. Daylilies proliferated wherever there had been people. Over the years we transplanted dozens of daylily roots to line the stone wall leading up to our farmhouse.

Digging in cellar holes became a favorite diversion for our kids. After spending the night in sleeping bags on the living room rug, Danny and his friends, sometimes

five or six of them, would go out and excavate these cav-
ities, turning up pottery shards, medicine bottles, and in
one site, presumably a cobbler's shop, the lasts of many
different sizes of shoes. Over time the boys also proved
to be a welcome source of free labor, hacking down
brambles, hauling dead logs out of the woods to be cut
up for winter burning, and lugging the dump-load gift
of railroad ties from an abandoned line into position for
the paddock we planned to attach to the barn.

Exploring the other side of town by car one rainy
day, we spotted a pasture full of Shetland ponies. Eleven-
year-old Judith, already in love with horses, had spent a
month the preceding summer living with the daughter of
one of my old college friends and learning how to ride.
We stopped to admire the nimble ponies and were warmly
received by their owner. The farm wasn't limited to ponies;
there were several riding horses as well, and they were
available for trail rides. The owner's daughter, Liz, provided lessons in a capacious outdoor ring that her husband,
Ted, had erected. My own passion for horses reawakened,
I began to take riding lessons over the ensuing months.
Soon, Victor joined me. Guided by Liz, we began to enjoy
riding the many trails on that side of the mountain.

Liz was planning to take in half a dozen girls the

following summer. Judith's fate was sealed. The group would live in a cabin that was just then being built out beyond the ring. Each girl would have a suitable horse or pony of her own for the season. Our friendship with Liz and Ted developed. Ted had restored and enlarged their old downhill barn, not unlike our own. The tough little ponies had free in-and-out access to the underneath area, much as we envisioned that the eventual transformation of our manure pit would provide for possibly two horses. (One winter there were to be seven. Like Liz, I found it hard to say no to hard-luck cases.) I remember that she took in somebody's unwanted donkey and turned him out with the ponies. They all nestled together under the barn without incident until the donkey brayed. Alarmed ponies sprayed out in all directions.

That first summer of riding camp Judith had a very pretty chestnut pony equally at home in harness and under saddle. They made a fine pair. In the fall Judith was able to join the local pony club that met weekends. The chestnut pony had been leased and would soon have to be returned to her owner; Liz and I began to haunt various horse auctions in the vicinity. It was her eagle eye that spotted two good-size dappled gray ponies a Maine farmer had bought for his sons. The boys preferred tractors to equines and their father was eager to unload the geldings as a pair. Victor was on board with buying a pony; when I came in that night after probably three earlier forays, he was already asleep. He woke up long enough to ask, "Did you buy a pony?" but heard only the first part of my reply, "No. I bought two." In the morning he learned that we were now owners of Star and Dusty, approximately four and five years old. Dusty proved to be a talented jumper and placed in enough local shows and gymkhanas to plaster Judith's room with ribbons. When we went trail riding, I outfitted Dusty with our one saddle and she rode Star bareback.

And then it snowed. Of course it had snowed in Newton year after year, but this New Hampshire snow was deep, silent, reverenced. It gave rise to "The Presence":

Something went hard and slow
over our hayfield.
It could have been a raccoon
lugging a knapsack,
it could have been a porcupine
carrying a tennis racket,
it could have been something
supple as a red fox

dragging the squawk and spatter
of a crippled woodcock.
Ten knuckles underground
those bones are seeds now
pure as baby teeth
lined up in the burrow.

I cross on snowshoes
cunningly woven from
the skin and sinews of
something else that went before.

Virtually every pickup truck sported a plow nose.
Cars went by with skis attached to their racks. Snow-
mobiles buzzed along the woods trails. The town kept
our road open, but because it was steep and narrow and
involved negotiating two curves, it could be plowed only
by the grader, a monstrous apparatus. Only one special
town worker was permitted to operate it. The stone wall
on the barn side of the road loomed perilously close, as if
asking to be dislodged. Frequently a few stones lay strewn
against the shoulder and had to be set aside till spring.

Victor organized the family skiing expeditions. We
lived within easy reach of three ski areas that offered

The Pawnbroker's Daughter

lessons and bargain rates for season's passes. The kids mastered the beginners' slope in no time; Jane, our oldest, was especially adept. I struggled to graduate from the awkward but safe downhill snowplow to the more graceful stem turn, and then to the elegance of parallel skiing, carving U-turns across the slopes. No one else in the family incurred any injuries, but in my fourth season, executing a parallel turn over a mogul on the last run of the day, I fell and fractured my left leg. It was set at the local hospital by the doctor on call, a dermatologist. By the time we returned to the city that night, my toes had swollen to large purple orbs. My leg had to be reset by an orthopedic surgeon in a Boston hospital.

That first spring we had begun to refer to our weekend and holiday outings as going up-country. (I had no premonition that *Up Country* would become the name of my fourth collection of poems and go on to win a Pulitzer Prize.) One chilly April day we tramped around a swampy area a hundred yards above the house that was full of yellow flowers. They were my first marsh marigolds. When Henry called them cowslips, "The Vision of Sir Launfal" came back to me. I had memorized James Russell Lowell's poem in grammar school and here it was: "the cowslip startles in meadows green."

That it was an edible plant, and that the leaves, boiled in a change of two waters, were commonly served as a spring tonic, was another piece of country lore. But no one at supper would eat the dish and even I had to admit it was bitter. My experiments with nettle soup and milkweed in all three stages—sprouts, buds, and pods—fared no better. But fiddlehead ferns were a success.

Victor was not thinking about cowslips. After inspecting the marsh from an engineer's perspective, he got in touch with the New Hampshire soil conservation agency to discuss the possibility of digging a pond on the site. An actual private swimming hole would add sparkle to our Hope Diamond. A surveyor from the agency arranged for four test holes to be dug to see if the area contained any underground springs. It did. After all the trees had been cut and the marsh was cleared, excavation began the following summer. I remember trudging uphill with a cold beer for the bulldozer operator every noon for eight days. As the pond, two-thirds of an acre, neared completion, Ray conferred with us from his dozer. The drawings called for a six-foot-wide flat boulder to be removed from the shoreline. Ray suggested leaving it in place as a diving rock. For safe entry he would scoop out a hole ten feet deep in front of it.

We agreed. Thirty years later I described it in "Summer Meditation" as

the great rock
that is always dark
on its underside
the one I used to dive
from, aiming to come up
in the heart
of a cold spring
rising exultant
time after time
into the fizz
of lime-green light.

It took the rest of the year for the pond to fill. To my astonishment the water level rose exactly to the red stakes the surveyor had placed around the perimeter. Victor was gratified but not surprised; he had a scientist's faith in precision that I lacked. By the following summer we'd had a truckload of sand delivered and were requiring every swimmer to spread ten shovelsful before diving in. Soon we had a beach broad enough for a few folding chairs.

The day that Ray brought his bulldozer down the hill to load onto a flatbed trailer, he stopped at the house to talk to Victor. The well behind the house sat on a downhill slope; it seeped underground about fifty feet, then emerged in a damp circle. Ray proposed scooping this area out as a bonus to provide an emergency water source. It had never occurred to me, though it may have to Victor, that we were half a mile from a usable stream and a mile from access to a town hydrant. We've never, heaven forfend, needed this fire pond but are grateful for its presence. From late March till late summer, however, we are so noisily serenaded by tree frogs that we have to close the windows on that side of the house. Total cost for Ray's eight days of digging: $1,800.

The pond above the house became the epicenter of our up-country haven. Our customary attire was come-as-you-are, an abandonment I celebrated much later in "Skinnydipping with William Wordsworth," which opens,

> I lie by the pond *in utter nakedness*
> thinking of you, Will, your epiphanies
>
> . . .
>
> *Fair seed-time had my soul,*
> you sang; what seed-times still to come?

...

I lay my "Prelude" down under the willow.
My old gnarled body prepares to swim
to the other side.
                    Come with me, Will.

One sultry July day a Nobel laureate in science who
had audited a poetry course I was teaching once a week at
MIT paid us a visit. We invited him to join us in a cool-
ing dip. "One thing, though," Victor cautioned him as we
walked to the beach. "We generally swim in the nude."

"My wife is Swedish!" he cried, tearing off his
clothes.

A contest developed: who would swim earliest in
spring? Danny on a dare jumped in one St. Patrick's
Day. Who would be the last one in the fall? I won this
on an unrecorded late September afternoon, described
in "Summer Meditation":

... naked, pale
I slip between
two shores
of greenery
solitary

back in the muck
of womb while
there goes mr. big
the brookie
trailed by mrs. big
wispy silhouettes
darting in synchrony ...

Every other year Victor restocked the pond with brook trout; no fisherman himself, he didn't want to lose them all to river otters in one fell swoop. Only once in its fifty-year tenure has the pond entertained a family of *Lontra canadensis*. Spectacular swimmers, they were great fun to watch, but Victor was ambivalent about them. He had similar mixed feelings about the perennial great blue heron who posed like a statue on the dam, interrupting his seeming trance from time to time only to snag an unsuspecting fingerling, salamander, or frog. And then there were the kingfishers who took great exception to our presence and swept back and forth over our heads, berating us with their rattling call. A wide assortment of dragonflies in paintbox colors fluttered and swooped past all summer. Spring and fall we were visited by migrating waterfowl, from mallards and mergansers to occasional wood ducks. There was always something to watch and exclaim over. Toward winter we kept the sand raked so that we could tell when our resident moose had strolled past, leaving his enormous twin half-moon hoofprints for us to admire.

Wild turkey tracks were commonplace all over the farm. In season mother turkeys would lead parades of their ten or twelve fluffy little ones. Many, even most of these, would be picked off one by one by predators. Nature red in tooth and claw. Reading about their mating habits, I stumbled on the term that opens "Discrete Activities":

The cloacal kiss between turkeys
seemingly awkward, still
makes more turkeys.
Every morning

a trail of poults in tow,
the wild flock courses
across the manure pile
to peck the redelivered seeds . . .

Clear-cutting two acres for the pond had also opened up a flat sunny spot for a vegetable garden.

Maxine Kumin

I had never grown anything more ambitious than a few store-bought petunia plants, but now I began to pore over catalogues and pamphlets about raising carrots and beets and green beans, onions and leeks and parsnips from seed. Our older daughter, Jane, was an enthusiastic participant. As we gradually grew more sophisticated, learning how to start seeds indoors in flats, then hardening them off first on the porch, then on the terrace, finally conveying them up to the garden at the appropriate time, she took over most of the tedious transplanting and weeding. But the first year we lost much of our produce to what proved to be a wily adversary, the woodchuck. Not one woodchuck, a creature we had never encountered before, but an extended family, a colony of rapacious nibblers and diggers. The hardware store owner advised chicken-wire fencing. He told us to bury it a foot deep. First we discovered that the soil was full of stones we learned to call New England potatoes. Then we discovered that the average woodchuck can tunnel under twelve inches of chicken wire overnight. Next, he suggested cyanide bombs. Inevitably, "Woodchucks" became the title of a poem that opens,

Gassing the woodchucks didn't turn out right.
The knockout bomb from the Feed and Grain Exchange
was featured as merciful, quick at the bone
and the case we had against them was airtight,
both exits shoehorned shut with puddingstone,
but they had a sub-sub-basement out of range.

We turned into killers, adept with the .22, not just
that one season. Not quite true; I never learned to shoot,
but some of our visitors and occasional handymen did.
It took three years to reduce the woodchuck popula-
tion to only rare sightings. As the vegetable garden
expanded, we installed raised beds and improved the soil
year by year with compost and aged horse manure. We
rebuilt the fence several times as it rusted, and ran a top
board around the perimeter for reinforcement. One of
our latter-day caretakers built an actual gate to replace
the makeshift stile we had been climbing over. One year
we installed plastic tubing to irrigate the rows by gravity
flow from the pond but had to abandon this method
as little salamanders kept getting stuck in the channels. When we added an adjoining raspberry patch and
started growing our own sweet corn, it became prudent

Maxine Kumin

to rig a double-strand electric fence that we energized when the berries ripened and the corn tasseled. It effectively said *Keep Out!* to raccoons and deer. Our garden became so fecund that we eventually bought a second freezer to contain the quantities of veggies and soups we put up for the year. But the real reason for our success lay with the by-product of our horses, described in this excerpt from "The Excrement Poem":

> We eat, we evacuate, survivors that we are.
> I think these things each morning with shovel
> and rake, drawing the risen brown buns
> toward me, fresh from the horse oven, as it were,
> . . .
> And wheeling to it, storming up the slope,
> I think of the angle of repose the manure
> pile assumes, how sparrows come to pick
> the redelivered grain, how inky-cap
>
> coprinus mushrooms spring up in a downpour.
> . . .
> [T]rundling off today's last barrowful
> I honor shit for saying: We go on.

It was the dailiness of tending an ambitious vegetable garden that captured me, "the rich assortment of
birds trilling on all / sides of my forest garden" where
I spread "sodden newspapers between broccolis, / corn
sprouts, cabbages and four kinds of beans," as described
in "Mulching." My 40-by-40 plot of black gold with
its orderly raised beds gratified me much as attending
the weekly Philadelphia Orchestra concerts in evening
dress must have gratified my mother.

> How can I help but admire the ever perseverant
> unquenchable dill
> . . . waving its lacy banners
> where garlic belongs or slyly invading a hill
> of Delicata squash—
> how can I help but admire such ardor? . . .

> Let me laud onion that erupts
> slim as a grass stem
> then spends the summer inventing its pungent tulip

I wrote in "An Insider's View of the Garden," and
declaimed at the end,

O children, citizens, my wayward jungly dears
you are all to be celebrated
plucked, transplanted, tilled under, resurrected here. . . .
For all of you . . .
I plan to spend the rest of my life on my knees.

The Old Harriman Place lodged deeper and deeper into our psyches. With a hired helper Victor undertook to cordon off the tumbled-in downhill side of the barn foundation to allow for a safe run-in space for future horses. A paddock went up with fence posts composed of the railroad ties mentioned earlier. We had recently met a retired Swiss couple who lived a mile away in a farmhouse dating back to the 1700s they had painstakingly restored. When they paid us a call just as the top boards of the five-foot-tall paddock fence were going up, the husband, Rudi, exclaimed, "My Gott! What you gonna keep in dere, elephants?" We hastily readjusted the dimensions.

Rudi and Margrit became not only our good friends but the source of counsel on everything from how to kill a porcupine—"chust step on his tail and hit him on the head with a two-by-four"—to the best local electrician and plumber to call. Rudi walked with Victor to the far corner of what eventually became our outermost pasture, the Elysian Field, and showed him our mutual boundary—"You begin here," he said, pointing backward, "and I begin dere," pointing forward. Margrit loved inviting our daughters for her famous hot chocolate drinks, and as soon as we had our own horses, they encouraged us to ride the woodland trail they had cleared between their property and the strawberry farm their cousin owned at the top of the rangeway. Margrit would stand at the back door of their house and wave as the horses and riders crested the hill, trotted by the site of the old mill, and came into view. It was Margrit who told me that ten years earlier, Henry's privy had been demolished and an indoor bathroom installed by Rudi. It was not the kind of thing Rudi would mention; he was just being a good neighbor.

We were still only weekenders and vacationers, though we agreed that at some point we would give up the house in Newton, move up-country, and live there year-round. I was more than ready. Victor, knowing a daily commute to Boston was impractical, held back. He didn't want me to live alone from Monday to Friday; if we converted the second floor of the barn to an apartment, we could rent it to tenants of our own choosing. We began to look for a builder.

Meanwhile, we had supper with Liz and Ted and their three kids on an occasional Saturday that had been full of horse activities; sometimes they came to our farm. Judith had practically moved in with them. She remembers one late afternoon after barn chores when Liz invited us all to join them. I had replied, "We'd love to. But I have six knockwurst for dinner. What shall I do with them?" "Oh, just bring them with you," Liz said. We left. Judith stayed to help. She found Liz rooting around in the big freezer in the pantry and asked, "What are you doing?"

"Your mother is bringing six friends and I'm trying to figure out what to feed them."

I thought about this dialogue long after. I thought about the rigid formality of Saturday night dinners in Newton, the polished silver candlesticks, the ironed tablecloths, the fancy desserts, and how seamlessly and graciously Liz's invitation had been extended. Our Monday-through-Friday schedules were rigorous; Victor commuted to Boston to the engineering firm that employed him. Sometimes he traveled to assess projects in North Carolina or Texas. Two afternoons a week I taught two freshman English classes at Tufts University just outside Boston, one to dental technicians, the other to phys ed majors. Mornings, once the kids were off to school, I hurried through housework to my desk, where I worked on poems. Anne Sexton and I read drafts to each other over the phone. We were published in the major magazines. Despite the general dismissal of women's poetry as merely domestic, each of us had three books to our credit.

Winning the Pulitzer Prize for my fourth book was wonderful, but it filled me with anxiety. Being in the limelight terrified me. It was well known that fame often led to writer's block. At that moment I dreaded the paralysis I was certain awaited me. Would I ever write again? As soon as I could, I fled to the farm. There I took Candide's advice to cultivate my garden and started the season's first crop of frost-hardy chard, lettuce, and spinach. I dug compost into the soil, raked, gathered bucketsful of stones, raked again. Once I had dirt packed under my fingernails I recovered my equilibrium. The poems inched back in their own time.

V.

The Making of PoBiz Farm

Approaching PoBiz Farm up the steeply curved
dirt road, winter 2014. *Susannah Colt*

Through our first-ever covered bridge, up a steeply curving dirt road, we suburbanites came with three children to an abandoned farm. Here, where I grew as a poet, we became true New Englanders, with a vegetable garden, a pond, a barn full of horses, and a succession of shelter dogs.

How much my life had changed since that fateful drive in 1961. After the Pulitzer Prize in 1973, I metamorphosed into a recognizable name. Invitations came my way to give readings, teach a class, be poet-in-residence for a week, a month, a semester. I could pick and choose. Travel expenses were reimbursed and honoraria paid; suddenly I was in business, the poetry business.

That same year Victor found a contractor willing to

undertake the dicey job of shoring up the barn foundation so that we could use the whole space. Before then,
we had room only for two mares leased for riding and,
over one summer vacation, two of a neighbor's weanling
foals unrelated to the mares. The entire underpinning of
unwieldy boulders that had shifted and rolled loose was
to be replaced with poured concrete.

It was heavy work and slow going. We almost lost
the contractor and the barn when one section collapsed
while he was on the job. We also had a new well dug to
serve the barn and an apartment we planned to build on
the top floor. This enabled the contractor to run a water
line through the rear wall into the narrow space that
would serve as sawdust bin and grain room. (We were
to experience a thousand regrets over the ensuing years
that we hadn't insulated the line. Every time it froze,
one of us would have to squat, sometimes for more than
an hour, holding a hair dryer aimed at the faucet.) A
year later we had six rustic but serviceable stalls, all built
by Victor and a hired hand. Two of them are extra large
for foaling, and a narrow stall at the back was designed
to hold sawdust to be used as bedding. The arrangement
left a twenty-foot-wide rectangle allowing the horses
free access in and out. A friend named it the motel

lobby. Another friend made a sign that still hangs on the lip of the haymow facing the house: POBIZ FARM. For a couple of amateurs who had so much to learn about breeding and raising our own horses, the farm was a costly indulgence. The poetry business helped to support it.

Victor and I put our suburban Boston house on the market and early in 1976 became permanent New Hampshire residents. For more than a decade we had camped out with our three children in the farmhouse. Now we left the comforts of central heating for wood-stoves, dependable wattage for frequent power outages due to storms, and shades in every window, as well as downstairs curtains, for a wide-open lifestyle. Drafts blew in around the loose windows. There were windy gaps between the baseboards and the floor. We had an RFD address, a mailbox at the foot of the hill, a phone with a party line. At our first primary election in the town hall, we requested Democratic ballots, which had to be hastily hunted up, and survived unscathed in what was then a staunchly Republican district. We now owned two mares and had taken in a homely roan gelding named Jack who had broken out of his lonely nearby quarters several times and gone wandering in search of equine companionship. A careful fellow, Jack always stayed on the edge of the county road, as his footprints attested. Since one of our mares had been bred, we would soon need a second mount for our initiation into the new sport of competitive trail riding. Jack's owner was happy to part with him.

Our local trail riders association sponsored a 25-mile event describing a circle on the other side of town. Like a road rally, there was a window of time within which participants had to finish. Horses were judged on their general fitness at completion. We were hooked. Over the next eleven years, our weekends from May through October were spent on trail rides—one to three days in duration and 25 to 100 miles long—all over New England. Our stalls filled, indeed overfilled. One year Jack lived contentedly in the motel lobby. In the poem "Jack," I described him as

. . . Wise old campaigner, he dunks his

hay in the water bucket to soften it, then visits the others who hang their heads over their Dutch doors. Sometimes he sprawls out flat in his commodious quarters.

What I found rewarding about this sport, as opposed to the show world of dressage and jumping, was how naturally the horses took to it. They were being used in accord with their basic instincts, moving in a group— willing, well-behaved athletes outfitted with lightweight saddles and simple snaffle bits. I attended seminars on horse care, breeding, and foaling and signed up for clinics on the horse-whisperer methodology that is gradually replacing Wild West bronc-busting techniques.

Victor and I went for long rides to keep our horses fit, exploring the Mink Hills on overgrown trails to the site of a settlement that once warranted a schoolhouse—long gone. The dogs went everywhere we went. In "Gus Speaks," our second Dalmatian tells his own long-lived story.

I was the last of my line,
farm-raised, chesty, and bold.
Not one of your flawless show-world
forty-five-pound Dalmatians.
I ran with the horses, my darlings.

I loped at their heels, mile
for mile, swam rivers they forded

wet to the belly. I guarded
them grazing, haloed in flies.
Their smell became my smell.

. . .

Now I lie under the grasses
they crop, my own swift horses

who start up and spook in the rain
without me, the warm summer rain.

We bought a used horse trailer and spent weeks teaching our horses how to go calmly in and out. We bought a truck outfitted to pull a trailer. We spruced up the springhouse to serve as living space for a summer horse girl and were deluged with aspirants. Our first horse girl had just graduated from Dartmouth, where she had been captain of the equestrian team. She brought her own horse with her and left us a year later to get married. The horse girl position eventually morphed into farm caretaker. Our present caretaker Susannah (Suzy) Colt had been our horse girl in 1983; she left us to go to law school, spent several productive years representing women in domestic abuse cases, and came back to look after the farm and its aging inhabitants.

Our first foal was born in 1976 to a mare who had been used in a cocaine drug scam, confined for six months in a trailer. We bought her from the slaughterer for 30 cents a pound and bred her to an undersized Arabian stallion with a clubfoot. The stud fee was $50. That foal, Boomer, lived to the august age of thirty-five. She had a successful career as Victor's 100-mile horse before we retired her to use as a broodmare. Her first foal, named Praise Be, led to this poem of the same name:

Eleven months, two weeks in the womb
and this one sticks a foreleg out
frail as a dowel quivering
in the unfamiliar air and then
the other leg, cocked at the knee
at first, then straightening
and here's the head, a big blind fish
thrashing inside its see-through sack
and for a moment the panting mare
desists, lies still as death.

I tear the caul, look into eyes
as innocent, as skittery

as minnows. Three heaves, the shoulders pass.
The hips emerge. Fluid as snakes
the hind legs trail out glistering.
The whole astonished filly, still
attached, draws breath and whinnies
a treble tremolo that leaps
in her mother who nickers a low-key response.

Let them prosper, the dams and their sucklings.
Let nothing inhibit their heedless growing.
Let them raise up on sturdy pasterns
and trot out in light summer rain
onto the long lazy unfenced fields
of heaven.

Having a foal in the oven shortens the winter in
a way unmatched by any other. Nothing takes the bite
out of a New England February like the daydream of a
new youngster on spindly legs racing across the pasture
in midsummer. We prepared well in advance, filling the
narrow stall at the back of the barn to the brim with
green pine sawdust. The reason for my vigilance was
a stillbirth with no one in attendance many years ago.

Afterward I realized that from our bedroom I had heard a kick in the barn but didn't rouse myself to investigate. Presumably the caul over the foal's nose never ruptured, and the bewildered first-time mother didn't intervene. Some things we can never forgive ourselves for.

Traditionally, a week before due date I moved down, spreading my sleeping bag on top of the sawdust pile and hanging a trouble light from a hook over my head so that I could read between dozing and waiting for the first restless sounds made by a mare going into labor in the adjoining stall. Victor had rigged an intercom so that I could call him; he could pull on sweatpants and boots and get down to the barn in ninety seconds. He was calm and sensible. I was invariably in a state of exalted terror, focused on all the things I learned at clinics that can go wrong. Our vet was almost an hour away. Even though I'd never had to open them, I had a package of sterile, elbow-length plastic gloves ready. A squirt bottle of iodine was at hand to sterilize the umbilicus. The mare was wearing an old leather halter we kept for this occasion. (Unbreakable nylon halters are accidents waiting to happen.)

I had learned to doze through snuffling and snorting sounds, arisings and lyings-down, and how to come abruptly awake at the final unmistakable sounds of beginning labor. But there's more to it than that, aspects I have tried to describe in this excerpt from "Sleeping with Animals":

> Nightly I choose to keep this covenant
> with a wheezing broodmare . . .
> who grunts in her sleep in the vocables
> of the vastly pregnant. . . .
> I in my mummy bag just outside her stall
> observe the silence, louder than the catch
> in her breathing, observe gradations of
> the ancient noneditorial dark;
>
> . . .
>
> What we say to each other in the cold black
> of April, conveyed in a wordless yet perfect
> language of touch and tremor, connects
> us most surely to the wet cave we all
> once burst from gasping, naked or furred
> into our separate species.

Most mares foaled at night; probably in their undomesticated state they took advantage of the cover of darkness. But one of our mares delivered her foal in midmorning out in our farthest field, surrounded by the rest of the herd. By the time we found her, she was back on her feet, it was raining, and Jack was trying to lick the foal dry. We had to make several trips to remove the terribly curious nonparents from the vicinity. Then we led the gentle Quarter Horse mare across five acres of pasture and down a craggy hillside to the barn. The hours-old baby bopped along merrily, unfazed.

In the winter of 1979, I rescued another horse. Medas Genesis—I called her Gennie—was a Standard-bred who had failed at the track. She had been confined in a space just wide enough to turn around in, and when she came to us, she had barely enough muscle left to walk into the trailer. A month later I took her with me to New Jersey, where I was teaching a poetry workshop at Princeton for a semester. I boarded her at a 600-acre estate half an hour from the university where she shared an enormous pasture with a dozen Welsh ponies. Every morning I taught my seminar and every afternoon I drove out to ride Gennie.

This experiment was so successful that in 1981, when I was U.S. Poet Laureate, I took five-year-old

Boomer with me to Washington. At six every morning
I drove against the flow of traffic to Potomac, Maryland,
where Boomer was the queen of three adoring hunt club
geldings. (No live foxes were involved; the club dragged
an artificial scent.) I fed the foursome, mucked out, rode
my mare, and made it back to the Library of Congress
by eleven.

Finding a temporary home for Boomer in the
D.C. area was serendipitous; the preceding August at
the Bread Loaf Writers' Conference in Middlebury,
Vermont, I had met a psychiatrist poet-wannabe from
Potomac. He and his wife had an empty box stall and
an eight-acre field just thirty minutes from Capitol
Hill, and he offered it in exchange for my help with his
manuscript.

I have explained earlier that it took me several
years to accept a position at Bread Loaf. I was simply
too intimidated by the big names. Finally I became
a staff member in 1969, and returned in subsequent
years half a dozen times for two weeks in mid-
August. At Bread Loaf I made some lifelong friends.
Well before my time, Robert Frost himself was a frequent visitor at the staff house. His presence there was

mythic and inspired this imaginary encounter in "The Final Poem":

. . . don't sit

there mumbling in the shadows, call
yourselves poets? All
but a handful scattered. Fate

rearranged us happy few at his feet.
He rocked us until midnight.
. . .
Reaching for the knob of his cane
he rose and flung this exit line:
Make every poem your final poem.

The mountainous woods around Bread Loaf were superb for foraging for wild mushrooms. I had already earned a reputation as a mycophagist when assistant director Sandy Martin and I were observed raising a ladder on campus to bring down a good array of oyster mushrooms growing on a tree. On rainy days Ciardi would tap his glass at lunch and announce, "The Witch of Fungi will lead a mushroom walk at three p.m." In Treman House, the staff retreat where faculty convened for preprandial drinks, we sautéed our chanterelles and oyster mushrooms to accompany our martinis. A goodly amount of drinking went on later in the lubricious evenings as well. Bread Loaf was known in some circles as Bed Loaf.

Foraging for mushrooms had attracted me years before we first glimpsed our farm. What fascinated me was nature's bounty, the chance to reap where you did not sow. I took a course offered by the Boston Mycological Society, found mushroom books in the local library, and eventually collected a dozen handbooks to contrast and compare pictures. I knew enough to obey two cardinal rules: never mingle species and never pick any mushroom with white gills—the underpart of the cap—for fear of unknowingly gathering the destroying angel, deadliest of the *Amanita*.

The first mushroom we actually ate was the shaggy mane *Coprinus*, sometimes called the lawyer's wig, with delicate gray gills that turn black and melt—deliquesce—as the fungus ages. It was plentiful and proved serviceable, if not outstanding, for soup. Guests from the city were wary; would they or wouldn't they? Eating wild mushrooms was exotic and dangerous. We persevered. By midsummer clusters of yellow flute-like chanterelles appeared along the woods roads and were even more visible from horseback. We treasured them simply sautéed or in omelets.

By September mushrooms were everywhere in the forest. Oyster mushrooms growing on dead or dying trees became our favorites. One afternoon, while I was riding with a friend, a rich clump growing well above our heads came into view. I dismounted and held both horses' bridles while my companion stood up on her saddle like a circus acrobat to pluck the tree clean. We picked and enjoyed the distinctive yellow-orange sulfur polypore known as chicken-of-the-woods, as well as half a dozen other mushrooms. In "The Dreamer, the Dream" I described *Armillaria mellea*, where the dreamer comes

> upon great clusters of honey mushrooms
> breaking the heart of old oak ...
> a hundred caps grotesquely piggyback
> on one another, a caramel mountain
> all powdered with their white spores

... and all this they do in secret ...
lumbering from their dark fissure
going up like a dream going on.

Since species tend to regrow in the same locales year
by year, we triumphantly reaped annual crops where we
had not planted, tended, or tilled. Alas, the prized morel
has turned up only once despite our ardent searches.

Another crop we hadn't tended grew in heavy
clumps around the back of Henry Manley's house a half
mile away. I described it in "Extrapolations from Henry
Manley's Pie Plant": "The stalks as thick as cudgels, red
/ as valentines, a quarter-acre bed."

He told us to help ourselves. When I took him a
juicy rhubarb crisp, he allowed as how it wasn't half-bad.
But just as heavy frosts overtook the mushroom season,
Henry Manley, too, succumbed. First he moved in with
neighbors who looked after him in exchange for his
Social Security check. Then, as he grew frailer, a place
was found for him in a nursing home, where he died
after three months. His untended house had filled with
porcupines and dry rot and had to be razed. The new
property owners, Bonnie and Gary, first constructed a
big two-story barn; the box stalls suggested that they

intended to have horses. While they built a modest new house on the exact footprint of the old, they were living in a trailer with two young daughters, a dog, two cats, and a parakeet. Their vet asked them to take a four-month-old mutt he had been ordered to put down; its owners had confined the puppy to a second-story porch all day and complained that when they came home from work, he was too hyper to deal with. Bonnie and Gary took him in, but the trailer felt very crowded. Would we?

He was part spitz, part a jumble of other breeds, his name was Joshua. Amiable Gus, our resident dog, folded the puppy in like a playtoy, even tolerating having him hang onto his jowls as they ran downhill behind us when we set out on horseback. Every day Joshua revisited his prior digs, trotting back home with a talisman from Bonnie and Gary's barn: a child's rubber boot, a curry-comb, a mangled halter (by then the family had acquired a Shetland pony), once, to my initial horror until I could see it wasn't human, a big baby doll. His finest hour came when he trudged uphill with a pair of ice skates tied together. Lugging them by the laces, he progressed twenty feet, then set his burden down to catch his breath, then proceeded *doggedly*. After that, a door was installed at the top of the steps leading to the barn storage area.

Gus and his littermate Claude had come to us two years after we made the final move to PoBiz Farm, and they ran together like a pack. The only way to keep them on the premises was to chain one of them at a time, and this made us all unhappy. We gave Claude to a poet and his wife, who subsequently gave him away; I never heard what Claude's ultimate fate was. That guilt haunts me as does Jack's, from the poem that bears his name.

> That spring, in the bustle of grooming
> and riding and shoeing, I remember I let him go
> to a neighbor I thought was a friend, and the following
>
> fall she sold him down the river. I meant to
> but never did go looking for him, to buy him back
> and now my old guilt is flooding this twilit table.

Although Gus had thrived as an only dog, he tended to hang out with the horses. He and Joshua got on well together, but they never showed any impulse to bond as a pair and wander off without us. We were startled and then alarmed twelve years later when Gus disappeared. We put ads in the local lost-and-found columns, hung posters downtown, alerted everyone we knew that he was missing. I had a nagging worry I kept to myself: that winter a trapper had requested permission to set traps on our land. I had refused but perhaps none too politely. Two weeks later I spotted, floating on the far side of the pond, what I at first mistook for a white birch log with black markings. It was Gus's body. Now I feared the worst. I pulled off my shoes, waded in the chilly April water fully clothed, then swam to his drowned form and tugged him back to the dam. His body was perfectly preserved. There were no marks of a trap, no visibly broken bones. He might have been frogging and had a heart attack, the kindest death I could imagine for him. Victor was in Texas that week. Bonnie and Gary came up the hill and helped me dig a grave on the berm of the pond where Gus had been the "Custodian." It was a sweet memory, but I wept over every shovelful.

> Enter our spotted dog.
> Every summer, tense with the scent of them,
> . . . he stalks his frogs . . . an old pensioner
> happy in his work.
> . . .
> Once every ten or so pounces
> he succeeds, carries his captive north

in his soft mouth, uncorks him on the grass,
and then sits, head cocked, watching the slightly
dazed amphibian hop back to sanctuary.

Over the years the pond's inhabitants
seem to have grown accustomed
to this ritual of capture and release.
They ride untroubled in the wet pocket
of the dog's mouth, disembark in the meadow
like hitchhikers, and strike out again for home.

A few weeks later I went to New York to attend the
annual banquet of the Academy of American Poets,
where I was getting an award. Each table had eight
place settings; one stood empty at our table. After the
opening remarks and fruit cup, Stanley Moss, the poet
and publisher of Sheep Meadow Press, arrived breath-
less and somewhat disheveled. Driving down the West
Side Highway from Riverdale, he had seen a collar-
less dog loose in traffic and watched it narrowly avoid
being struck several times. He pulled over, leapt from
his car, yanking his belt loose to use as a leash as he
pursued the dog. The captive was in his car, parked just
down the street.

Between the main course and dessert, my editor at Norton and I trooped out with Stanley to see what he had rescued: a big, skinny dog, part German shepherd, possibly part collie, was contentedly curled up on the backseat. He had to be neutered, wormed, given rabies and distemper shots, and treated for severe dehydration. Stanley and his wife Jane paid all the vet bills but found they could not make peace between their old dog and the newcomer. Would we? Once he was fit to travel, the Mosses drove up to New Hampshire with him. It was my turn to do the naming; years ago Victor had named the two barn cats Abra and Cadabra when I had lobbied for the Dickinson sisters Emily and Lavinia. I chose to name our new dog Rilke because he had been rescued by the angels that lurked in the poet's poems. Rilke instantly attached himself to Victor, forming a lifetime bond. He was polite and accepting of family members but barked at any vehicle or pedestrian who came up the hill, including meter readers, UPS drivers, and propane gas deliverers. Although he never growled, that black face conveyed a certain menace to strangers.

Our next needy dog came by way of our son's childhood friend. On a driving vacation with his wife in

Maxine Kumin

Xochiapulco, Mexico, they had taken in a small bedraggled terrier type, smuggled him back into the States, hid him in their no-pets-allowed apartment while they were house-hunting, only to be betrayed by a neighbor. Another late-night phone call: Would we?

Xochi proved admirable and easygoing. Both he and Rilke learned after one expensive encounter with a porcupine to keep their distance from all quilly pigs. Some dogs, our vet explained, go back immediately to do battle and can never be cured of the desire for revenge. We had to return a miniature dachshund to our equine vet after one hefty bill for quill removal; she found this little bundle of ferocity a new home with a fenced backyard.

We were used to 60-pound dogs who thumped their way into or out of a room; Xochi padded about as noiselessly as a cat. He moved from rug to chair to sofa to bed. *Down!* We drew the line at beds. But the life of "this part rat terrier, part / the kind of dog who lives in a lady's lap" came to a very sad end after only six years with us. He was attacked by a visiting dog, and although the three bites looked minor, by evening Xochi seemed troublingly lethargic. Medical crises, whether human or animal, invariably occur after office hours. We drove to the nearest emergency vet clinic twenty miles away and paid $100 up front before any evaluation took place. After a physical exam followed by X rays determined this was indeed a minor incident, we paid another $200 and drove home. The vet said she had given Xochi a light tranquilizer so that he could have a good sleep. I sat with him on the couch as his breathing slowed. He died an hour later in my arms. The attending vet insisted he must have had a preexisting condition and offered to perform an autopsy. We declined. The bitter taste this incident left in my mouth remains to this day.

We didn't know there were to be two more canine rescues heading our way. A hound dog was next. Virgil had had a hard history. His first owners had taken him in from Death Row, a kill shelter in Pennsylvania. The adoption went sour for reasons unknown and he was turned over to a different shelter. This time he was taken in by a Brooklyn family, friends of our daughter. Soon thereafter he pulled their dog walker down the front steps of their brownstone, breaking her jaw. The midnight phone call asked, Would we? We didn't especially want another dog so soon after losing the little guy who says, in the last lines of his sonnet "Xochi's Tale," "I dwell in heaven but without the wings," but how could I resist one bearing a poet's name? A city apartment was no place for a young hound dog; he needed space to run. The first time we opened the farmhouse door and invited him out he looked back at us in disbelief. Then he took off, nose down, across the pastures. After letting him out early every morning, we could hear him baying in the distance, making ever-wider circles around the farm, using his own built-in GPS. Virgil had his own sonnet, which ends,

> He longs for love with all his poet's soul.
> His eyebrows make him look intelligent.
> We save our choicest food scraps for his bowl.

What I said about no dogs on beds was not quite true. After a nearly fatal carriage-driving accident in 1998, I could no longer navigate the steep, uneven staircase to the second floor. Victor hired an architect to design an addition to the back of the house for me, a modern bathroom with stall shower and a combination study and bedroom. Once I moved into my new quarters, Virgil took possession of my twin bed butted up against Victor's.

I don't remember how we learned about the plight of Rosie, a 14-pound bundle of self-sufficiency, who was found with a human corpse and a dozen other dogs in the small town of Decatur, Tennessee. She came north steerage class in a tractor-trailer full of stacks of dogs in crates. We were told she had a slight heart murmur; only weeks after she arrived, she was diagnosed by our own trusted vet as being in congestive heart failure. She was ten years old and had spent her life either in a crate or on the concrete floor of a kennel, and knowledge of that helped us deal with the harsh reality that she might die at any minute. In actuality, this homely little mutt with bat ears and an anteater nose had three good years to race across the pasture, dabble in the pond, go fearlessly in and out of the horses' stalls while they were eating, tell Virgil where he could sit, and assume command of the household.

I have never been able to keep our animals, their births, eccentricities, and deaths, out of my poems. About a year after her lungs filled with water and Rosie was struggling to breathe, the vet euthanized her in my arms. We brought her home to take her place in the growing graveyard of overloved horses and dogs. My grief for this joyful life cut short surprised me with its intensity. Two years later I was able to assume her voice.

Rosie Speaks

shriven: to have obtained absolution

Now that I'm gone perhaps they'll forgive my sins—
those times I woke in the night and trotted
downstairs to relieve myself—not only of urine—
on the guest room rug; they'll allow me the junco I caught

and swallowed whole except for a last indigestible
feather; grant me the chipmunk that followed,
its tail protruding, until with a final gust
I managed to get it down, harshly swallowed.

Aren't these mere peccadilloes compared to my gifts?
When green beans were topped and tailed wasn't
I there to search and destroy the stray bits?
I was the secret snorkeler, the pointy-nosed peasant

who served under the table at meals, who leapt
into laps at leisure, or performed when the cue was given,
rolling over and over, delighting the guests.
Wasn't I ever the darling? Tell me I'm shriven.

Victor and I reached an unspoken agreement that we wouldn't take in any more waifs after Rosie. Just keeping PoBiz Farm up and running—stalls and pastures mucked out, fences in good repair, dead trees chainsawed and stacked, garden composted, planted, and tended daily—required extra help. The poetry business was in full swing, which meant I was spending a lot of time away from the farm. We hired a wonderful quasi-Buddhist caretaker who stayed with us for four years before retiring. His successor was Kevin, a former state policeman who, in addition to his many skills with guns (translation: porcupine eradication), chainsaws, and machinery in general, was a comfortable companion on horseback. By then Boomer had been diagnosed with Cushing's disease, a disorder of the pituitary gland common in older horses, and deemed no longer safe to ride. My good friend, the journalist and author Ann Jones, needed a home for her aging white gelding named Sailor, a bombproof horse who would stand directly under sheets of snow cascading off the barn roof while the others flew out to pasture in terror. We were happy to offer him a home. Kevin would boost me up from the mounting block to Sailor's broad back, he would swing onto Deuter, the horse I loved and who came so close to ending my life in 1998 in the freak driving accident, and we would go for a decorous half-hour walk-and-trot.

From 1998 on I suffered constant neuropathic pain but learned to live with it; at least I was back in the saddle for a few years. Then Deuter's nosebleeds began. Losing him to cancer of the sinuses was devastating. I described in "The Taste of Apple" that I had seen this handsome chestnut gelding into the world twenty-six years ago when he "staggered to his feet / with only a few false lunges in the predawn black and suckled / in small audible gulps from his warm mother." Now

> I stood with him feeding
> him apple slices slowly slowly making them last
>   ...when

> [the vet] shot the syringe full of pentobarb into
>   his vein. He dropped
> with a thud, a slain king ...

the taste of apple wasting in his mouth.

Only two horses remained. Our needs had changed; we needed someone capable of taking on regular house-keeping chores along with the daily horse care, the garden, and seasonal mowing. Kevin was ready to retire. We parted friends, and Suzy, newly retired from lawyering, returned to the farm.

In 1991 I was asked to provide an entry for a Festschrift in celebration of the poet May Sarton's eightieth birthday. It seems even more apt today than it did when I composed it in my youthful sixty-fifth year.

When I think of growing older—
suddenly, one is sixty, then, incredibly,
seventy, miraculously, eighty!—I think
of a term equestrians use to describe
changing from one gait to a higher one.
It is called making an upward transition.
    Mid-autumn, when the weather turns
brisk, our horses can't seem to make an
upward transition without inserting a
buck or two. We avoid using the word
canter that incites, and fall back instead

on a code. As a hill approaches, one rider may say to another, "Would you like to watermelon up this?" We hope to depart from the trot in a seemly manner, as bucks are quite contagious, horse to horse.

Certainly our human desire is to make all our upward transitions in a seemly fashion. We need neither code words nor euphemisms. When we hurt, we hurt. When we fall sick, we name the disease. And when we can get from day to day with some relish, we deserve to congratulate ourselves.

It's the upward transition that holds me fast. I make a point of looking across to the POBIZ FARM sign on the front of the haymow. What do I want for it after we're gone, all but 30 of its 200 acres conserved with the New Hampshire Forest Society? I don't expect it to be handed down in the family; the grown children have other lives, other responsibilities. But my hope is that the farm will again fill with horses. That some unwanted

dogs will be welcomed here and know love. That the
ghost of Boomer, whose great age let me almost think
her immortal, will return where she

gleams like a waxed

Mercedes. Canters
uphill to pasture,

trots down.
I try to imagine

the sweet tasseled fields
without her

the blind glass of midnight
without her

peremptory whinnies
to summon the others

when lightning
shatters it,

the way
the little herd will

close around her absence,
the way they'll go

on grazing, mouths slobber-
full of the last clover.

The last two horses of Maxine and Victor's lives,
"still noble to look upon," winter 2011. *Susannah Colt*

Acknowledgments

This collection includes four previously published essays:

"Love in Wartime": *The American Scholar* (Autumn 2012)

"Metamorphosis: From Light Verse to the Poetry of Witness": *The Georgia Review* (Winter 2012)

"Our Farm, My Inspiration": *The American Scholar* (Winter 2014)

"The Making of PoBiz Farm": *The American Scholar* (Spring 2014)

Poems Cited

Page 87: "Heaven as Anus" (*House, Bridge, Fountain, Gate*, 1971)

Pages 87–88: "Lines Written in the Library of Congress after the Cleanth Brooks Lecture" (*Our Ground Time Here Will Be Brief*, 1982)

Pages 88–89: "Cross-Country Skiing" (*Connecting the Dots*, 1996)

Pages 89–90 and 123: "Mulching" (*Still to Mow*, 2007)

Page 91: "Red Tape and Kangaroo Courts I" (*And Short the Season*, 2014)

Page 91: "Entering Houses at Night" (*Still to Mow*, 2007)

Page 91: "What You Do" (*Still to Mow*, 2007)

Page 97: "Life's Work" (*House, Bridge, Fountain, Gate*, 1971)

Page 98: "Nightmare" (*Halfway*, 1961)

Pages 101 and 103–4: "Country House" (*The Nightmare Factory*, 1970)

Pages 105–6: "Hello, Hello Henry" (*The Retrieval System*, 1975)

Pages 111–12: "The Presence" (*The Nightmare Factory*, 1970)

Pages 115 and 117–18: "Summer Meditation" (*Jack and Other New Poems*, 2005)

Pages 116–17: "Skinnydipping with William Wordsworth" (*The Long Marriage*, 2001)

Page 119: "Discrete Activities" (*And Short the Season*, 2014)

Page 121: "Woodchucks" (*Up Country*, 1972)

Page 122: "The Excrement Poem" (*The Retrieval System*, 1975)

Page 124: "An Insider's View of the Garden" (*Connecting the Dots*, 1996)

Pages 134 and 148: "Jack" (*Jack and Other New Poems*, 2005)

Page 135–36: "Gus Speaks" (*Connecting the Dots*, 1996)

Page 137–38: "Praise Be" (*Looking for Luck*, 1992)

Page 140: "Sleeping with Animals" (*Nurture*, 1989)

Page 143: "The Final Poem" (*Still to Mow*, 2007)

Pages 145–46: "The Dreamer, the Dream" (*Up Country*, 1972)

Page 146: "Extrapolations from Henry Manley's Pie Plant" (*The Retrieval System*, 1975)

Pages 149–50: "Custodian" (*Nurture*, 1989)

Pages 152 and 154: "Xochi's Tale" (*Still to Mow*, 2007)

Page 154: "Virgil" (*Still to Mow*, 2007)

Pages 156–57: "Rosie Speaks" (*And Short the Season,* 2014)

Pages 158–59: "The Taste of Apple" (*Where I Live,* 2010)

Pages 161–62: "The Unfinished Story of Boomer" (*Where I Live,* 2010)